GRAND ILLUSIONS

PAINT
VINTAGE

GRAND ILLUSIONS

PAINT
VINTAGE

A FOOLPROOF AND INSPIRING GUIDE
TO CREATING THE MODERN RUSTIC LOOK

NICK RONALD AND DAVID ROBERTS

R&R
PUBLISHING

First published in 2016 by R&R Publishing (Dorset).

R&R Publishing (Dorset)
PO Box 9125
Beaminster
Dorset
DT6 9EL
England

E: sales@randrpublishingdorset.com

Words, Pictures, Style & Design
by Nick Ronald & David Roberts

Edited by Joanna Copestick
Design Intervention by Meryl Lakin
Additional Photography by Alistair Burnside

A CIP catalogue record for this book is available from the British Library.

ISBN 978 1 5262 0329 8

Printed in England

contents

FOREWORD

It was as a new member of the team at Good Housekeeping, nearly 20 years ago, that I came across a book on paint and paint techniques. A review copy, fresh from the publishers, penned by these very same hands.

Grand Illusions – it's all in the name and it sounds as fresh now as it did, confidently heading the painted furniture revolution, back then in the 90's. It's the lure of French sophistication paired with a clean country undertone. Classic and refined meets understated. What this company doesn't know about paint really isn't worth knowing.

I recall our props cupboard at the magazine, a tardis-like room filled with promise for this aspiring deputy home editor as she rifled through offerings from the latest interior trends. I had walked into my dream job and this space represented a home stylist's heaven in the form of paint tester pots and half-finished how-to's, along with the ingredients of a myriad of home decoration stories.

Grand Illusions played a big part in those formative years. I had come to Good Housekeeping after a stint assisting an art director of formidable interior taste where their revered catalogues were a firm staple in our planning meetings.

When I first opened my shop Caravan, Grand Illusions appeared once more. This time in the form of French brocante inspired reproduction collections within my own displays, joining me on my retail journey and three shop premises later to my now virtual store at Caravan Style. Within this time I wrote books myself. Ironically, thinking back now, I see one title, "Flea Market Style", akin to the very essence of Grand Illusions. Another, "Modern Vintage Style", reminds me of their own, long-standing, aesthetic.

I have always admired Grand Illusions' holistic approach to the home decoration business. Nick and David's integrity shines further than catalogue copy and styling, product ranges and trade show stands. A visit to Grand Illusions' HQ is also a yearly culinary event, with flowers and food to match the taste of the occasion. I will always remember my first trip when Nick, true to his nature, kindly gave me a lift back to the station and we bonded over home décor rumination.

"Empowering people has been an extremely rewarding part of our business" write Nick and David. This couple knows no pretension or haughtiness, as so often seen in the world of interior design, only genuine passion for their product and an overpowering urge to share their knowledge and creativity.

I've now read "Paint Vintage" and I'm itching to experiment. To dress, distress and revamp. I now feel empowered to not only use paint but to make things to paint (and I mustn't forget to mention, the list of stockists is an interior stylist's gem).

If you want to start from scratch, or simply up-cycle, this book will take you through it. "Paint Vintage" is a valuable guide to paints and paint techniques for today's interiors. It's candid and up-to-date, considered and intentional, written by a couple who truly know what they are talking about.

"Paint Vintage" is for the paint enthusiast, the home decorator, the interior stylist and the shop owner. It's for the café, bar or restaurant owner. It's for anyone who can pick up a paint brush (or pay someone else to, though the self-satisfaction factor won't quite be the same, of course). And when you've got your own copy, a second will make a very good gift.

"It's all about the mix and all about the detail". It's inclusive and it's exciting. Thank you Nick Ronald and David Roberts, you've inspired me once again.

Emily Chalmers
Caravan Style

www.caravanstyle.com

FIRST WORDS

We cannot believe that it is nearly twenty years since our first book on paint and paint techniques was published. Today, the world is a very different place, not least because the way we glean information and inspiration has changed so dramatically – indeed, it is a little surprising that books such as this, even have a place in modern society. Obviously, we certainly hope that they do, else our hard work has been in vain. Just as incredible is the plethora of paint that is now available – even specialist types like Chalk or Milk Paint can be found on many high streets.

Never more than now has there been a taste for 'upcycling' as it has become known. Vintage style has become a huge decorating phenomenon and even the most contemporary of schemes often incorporates a treasured vignette as a nod to times gone by.

The power of paint should never be underestimated. This simple medium can transform a habitat in a matter of hours. In our painterly world, the prime purpose is to give new life to furniture but as you will see, once you grasp the basic premise, the world can be your preverbial oyster. In the pages ahead you'll discover our unique approach to using beautiful paint and some other decorating ideas too.

When our first book was published, we wrote, rather tongue in cheek, '*Just what you need, here's another paint effects book*'. Thankfully, it went on to sell over fifty thousand copies around the world. The same kind of sentiment could have been expressed when we relaunched our paint collection two years ago, after more than a decade of absence. Mercifully, this proved yet again that there is some kind of guardian angel out there, as our new paints have also been embraced with a passion we could never have thought possible.

For the past two years, we have been teaching our stockists all the things we learned when we were one of the country's largest purveyors of hand-painted furniture. This information has been received with universal relish and glee. Empowering people has always been an extremely rewarding part of our business.

With all this enthusiasm, we felt it was high time we returned to the world of publishing - to share with you some of our techniques that have stood the test of time, updated and refreshed. Above all, we wanted to illustrate how relatively easy it is to achieve a sophisticated and professional result, each and every time. Here it is then... our foolproof guide. Enjoy!

Nick and David

PAINT WAS TO CHANGE OUR LIVES FOREVER...

It's fair to say that paint has always been a passion of ours. Not surprising, given it was mostly responsible for shaping much of our career in the 1990s. Our first shop opened in December 1987, in St Margarets, near Twickenham and by the end of the decade (and before the wonders of the worldwide web), we had more than 85,000 customers on our database – for a smallish retailer this was quite astonishing!

Funnily enough, it all started with a book for IKEA. Not long after the *Homes & Gardens* feature, one of our customers, a fabulous lady called Meryl Lloyd, asked us to paint and distress an old armoire and then illustrate the techniques in a new book she was creating for the Swedish furniture giant, with her friend, Jo Copestick. Unbeknown to us, whilst we were doing the shoot, Meryl and Jo were busy telephoning all their publisher contacts, saying that they had found the next new 'talent' and by the end of the week, we had three book offers on the table.

We signed with Ebury Press and went on to write three books on paint techniques and interiors, that were published all around the world. This led to regular appearances on radio and television and a huge amount of editorial in all the major interiors magazines, like the piece opposite and including the prestigious French titles, *Côté Sud* and *Côté Ouest*.

Interestingly, the type of paint we used then and now, which by it's generic name would be known as a Milk or Chalk Paint, is currently enjoying a tremendous period of growth. It has been around for over 25 years but is only now reaching a far greater audience. This is due to the current trend to 'upcycle, re-invent and do-it-yourself '. This phenomenon is a typical by-product of hard economic times and is echoed by current media trends and the type of television programmes being made.

Back in those heady times our furniture business continued to grow and grow. At our peak, we had four shops and a thriving mail-order business. A customer could, at that time, order bespoke painted furniture by mail, no matter where they lived – which on reflection does sound a little unbelievable, even now. With our distinct pared-down taste, we became known as 'the pioneers of French Style in the UK'.

Alongside this, we started teaching people our techniques on paint courses that started in a small kitchen at the back of the furniture store - just 10 people at a time in this tiny space. By the end of the decade we had a specially created teaching facility, where every week up to 20 people would come and learn the same professional methods we used in our furniture painting studios.

Review from The Financial Times

1st February 1997

Brocante from the UK

Lucia van der Post discovers an evocative range of furnishings

Is it an illusion or is it authentic Provençal *brocante?* Or could it simply be that that particularly enchanting chair you saw in a smart home interiors magazine or that slightly battered but oh, so perfect armoire, was found at Grand Illusions?

Grand Illusions has developed a unique line of almost instantly available and accessible furniture and furnishing accessories that look as if they have just been discovered tucked away in a French village. Only the

especially cynical or experienced eye would guess that it is all being made in the north of England to the designs of the two English owners of Grand Illusions.

Part of the reason the furniture looks so authentically scruffy is that it is made from timbers and joists that are genuinely old. All of it is more than 100 years old and it comes from houses and buildings in the north. The paint techniques are specially designed to make sure that no piece ever looks as if it had just emerged shin-

ingly new from some high-tech emporium.

We are, you will have gathered, talking romantic here. This is not furniture for those who are addicted to Tom Dixon and Ron Arad, whose idea of furnishing a house revolves around experimentation and bold new materials. The whole collection – besides furniture, there are accessories of all sorts – has been, in the words of one of the owners, Nick Ronald, "truly, madly, deeply inspired by France, or to be more accurate, French Country Style".

It reeks of a certain *nostalgie* for ways of life that are fast vanishing even in *La France Profonde*, but that it has great charm it is hard to dispute.

If you have despaired of finding a traditional *armoire*, if you have long wanted a proper old-fashioned housekeeper's cupboard or a Love Seat *à la Monet*, then you will find these pieces in Grand Illusions' mail order catalogue.

The prices seem extraordinarily reasonable – pieces such as Monet's Love Seat, if found in a genuine antique shop, would sell for more than twice the sum that Grand Illusions is selling it for (£325). The housekeeper's cupboard (a bottom cupboard with doors and upper cupboard with four shelves with either wired or glazed doors) sells for £660 if in bare

wood or £795 if painted.

Monet's dining chairs (copies of those from his house at Giverney) are £100 each (in bare wood). All the furniture can be bought either in bare wood or painted in one of 34 colours (all traditional colours made from earth pigments and china clay which emulate the flat milk paints of the 19th century).

One of the most popular lines with those who work at home and dislike the high-tech look of much home office furniture are pieces that Grand Illusions has designed to have the practical function required (filing cabinets, desks and the like) but to look like domestic furniture. There are drawer plan chests, pedestal desks, drawer organisers and filing cabinets in either plain wood or painted with the colour-ageing technique and finished with "antiqued" handles and other fittings.

The accessories include stripy blue and white china, countrified urns, candles and garden appurtenances, rustic pottery and the like.

SEVENTY NINE

THE EDITORIAL WE RECEIVED BACK THEN WAS SIMPLY EXTRAORDINARY...

GRAND ILLUSIONS
Simply
STAIN

CRAQUELEUR SET

BROWN WAX
Cire Brune

CLEAR WAX
Cire Claire

CRAQUELEUR SET

BROWN WAX
Cire Brune

CLEAR WAX
Cire Claire

PAINT KIT No. 1
EVERYTHING YOU NEED TO GIVE A
SMALL PIECE OF FURNITURE THAT
CERTAIN *JE NE SAIS QUOI*

VINTAGE PAINT
VINTAGE PAINT
VINTAGE PAINT
VINTAGE PAINT
VINTAGE PAINT
VINTAGE PAINT
VINTAGE PAINT
VINTAGE PAINT

VINTAGE PAINT
VINTAGE PAINT
VINTAGE PAINT
VINTAGE PAINT
VINTAGE PAINT
VINTAGE PAINT
VINTAGE PAINT
VINTAGE PAINT

GRAND ILLUSIONS
VINTAGE PAINT
Peinture de Lait
FOR FURNITURE, WALLS & PAINT EFFECTS
• WATER-BASED • SELF-PRIMING • MATT

GRAND ILLUSIONS
VINTAGE PAINT
Peinture de Lait
FOR FURNITURE, WALLS & PAINT EFFECTS
• WATER-BASED • SELF-PRIMING • MATT

GRAND ILLUSIONS
VINTAGE PAINT
Peinture de Lait

GRAND ILLUSIONS
VINTAGE PAINT
Peinture de Lait

GRAND ILLUSIONS
VINTAGE PAINT
Peinture de Lait

GRAND ILLUSIONS
VINTAGE PAINT
Peinture de Lait

GRAND ILLUSIONS
VINTAGE PAINT

GRAND ILLUSIONS
VINTAGE PAINT
Peinture de Lait
FOR FURNITURE, WALLS & PAINT EFFECTS
• WATER-BASED • SELF-PRIMING • MATT

GRAND ILLUSIONS
VINTAGE PAINT

GRAND ILLUSIONS
VINTAGE PAINT

GRAND ILLUSIONS
VINTAGE PAINT

GRAND ILLUSIONS
VINTAGE PAINT

GRAND ILLUSIONS

GRAND ILLUSIONS
VINTAGE PAINT
Peinture de Lait

GRAND ILLUSIONS
VINTAGE PAINT
Peinture de Lait

GRAND ILLUSIONS
VINTAGE PAINT
Peinture de Lait
FOR FURNITURE, WALLS & PAINT EFFECTS
• WATER-BASED • SELF-PRIMING • MATT

GRAND ILLUSIONS
VINTAGE PAINT
Peinture de Lait

ABOUT THE PAINT...

The cornerstone of all our activity has of course been the paint – our unique and beautiful, chalky, milky flat paint, produced in a range of over 30 gorgeous historic colours, sourced from an international palette. As we said before, it became a passion and a huge part of our working life. However, by the end of the decade we had become disenchanted with living in London and moved to Dorset. To make this possible, we decided to become wholesalers instead of retailers, and franchised out our shops and furniture-painting business. Sadly, within a short time, the new franchise agreement was to flounder and the shops closed. By this time, we were heavily involved in our new venture and could not rescue the paint – we had to move on...

Excitingly though, in the summer of 2014, after an absence of 12 years, we decided to relaunch our wonderful paint – and so **Grand Illusions Vintage Paint** was born again.

Now you could be forgiven for thinking that surely everyone has their own paint range out there these days. To a degree this is true, especially with many of them being labelled 'Historical' or 'Traditional'. But here's the thing...

We're talking an entirely different type of paint – not one that merely emulates the historical colours of the past, but a paint that actually *replicates* the gorgeously creamy flat buttermilk paint of the 18th and 19th Century in its *ingredients* as well as its colour. As such, **Grand Illusions Vintage Paint** has some characteristics that enable it to perform very differently from those vinyl emulsions (to give them their technical name) that purport to be vintage, historic or traditional.

And therein lies the clue – this paint (and other true milk paint) does not contain the plasticky vinyl that is found in modern emulsions – it is made with natural earth pigments, chalk, clay and a very small amount of acrylic medium to bind it together, replacing the casein or milk from days gone by. This gives it a truly chalky, matt, breathable finish – perfect for walls, floors and furniture – the latter being highly suited to the shabby chic look that is so popular. Indeed, with **over 46% chalk**, we believe this paint has one of the highest chalk contents on the market today. It is also VOC free and thus very eco-friendly indeed, which is important.

The recipe for our paint was originally produced by an antique restorer we came to know. He would mix natural pigments with milk or casein before developing a more commercially viable product that still retained all the unique qualities of milk paint. He also graciously taught us his painting techniques and, together, we went on to create our first range of colours that perfectly suited our pared-down French style. These were the forerunners of our new collection today.

15

NOW HERE'S THE THING...

SHADES OF GREY. MIX HURRICANE WITH SOME
EARL GREY AND ADD A LITTLE BROWN WAX.
PURE STYLE.

MODERN RUSTIC

THE NEW IDYLL

Many years ago when we first started teaching, students would often ask, 'Is this just a fad ?' Our response would always be the same, 'Country Style has been with us for many years and is almost sure to continue, as it is a complete classic – it's just the name that will change...' Country Style was the genre given to our kind of work back then. And to a degree that is exactly what has happened... only it has embraced some other emerging styles along the way, such as Pure Vintage, Industrial Style, Shabby Chic and, dare we say, a defiant New Country. As a group of styles this seems to be what we identify with at the time of writing this new book – so, Modern Rustic it is...

With this free thinking spirit in mind, the style can incorporate many things – faded painted furniture is up there at the top, as are vintage pieces, vintage graphics and a complete industrial vibe that sits quite comfortably in the most modern of settings. Yet it is also a world where unique and unusual materials are used in decoration – corrugated iron, concrete, timber and, our old favourite, rust. We are all romantics after all.

In this first chapter we look at some rather stunning examples of the style. The photograph on the left, and indeed all those on the next eight pages, have been generously loaned to us by one of our eminent paint stockists, namely **Attic** of Hampton Hill, whose shop is on the outskirts of London, near to Hampton Court. The owners, Deborah and Alistair Burnside have a fantastic eye for all things vintage and they use the paint to its absolute best – on the walls, on reproduction furniture and on the cherished antique pieces they find on their travels. Rarely have we seen this executed with such exquisite taste. If you're ever in that part of the world, then do make a visit – or take a peek at their website **www.discoverattic.com** You'll certainly be inspired. Do take a look at the complete list of stockists at the end of the book. They will all have their own inspiring and wonderful stories to tell, for sure.

NEW COUNTRY

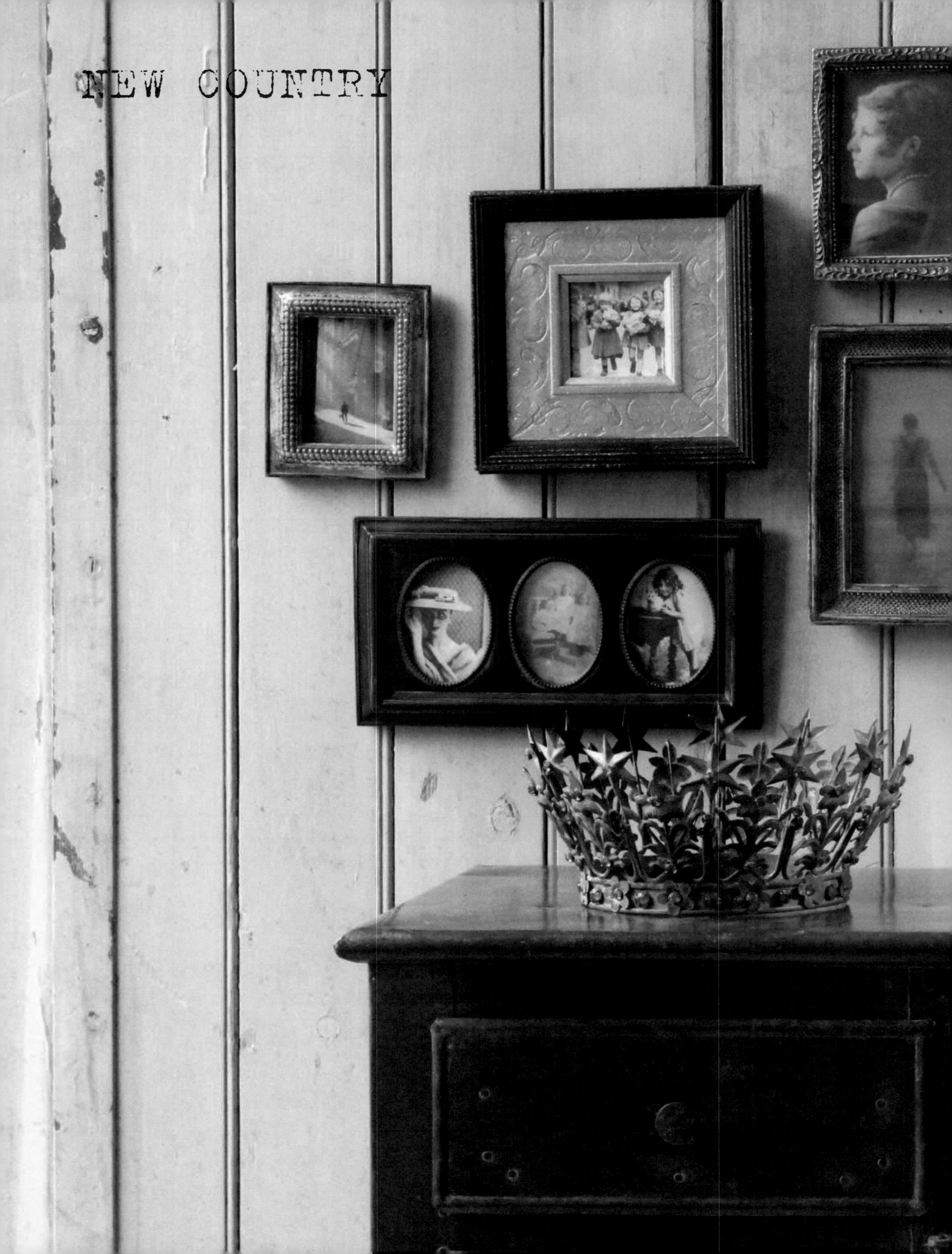

New Country, just like Modern Rustic,
embraces an eclectic mix of wonderful
'objets trouvés'. These are always a
completely personal statement as no two
people could ever create the same mix.
Here, we particularly love the fabulous
jewelled crowns. Although these are made
in India now, their origins are in fact
Mexican. They look wonderful, on top of
an old metal cabinet, set off against the
brilliant wood and metal door panels
behind, who could ask for more...

MODERN RUSTIC ELEMENTS

If you needed a
testament to just
stunning Vintage P
looks in-situ, t
look no further
Here, Attic have
the paint extensiv
The walls on this
are in Hurricane,
the chest in Sel
Mer, aged gently
brown wax.
Opposite above, a
beautiful
armoire painted
Charleston and
dresser in Shutt
while down below
little black numb
one-colour aged
Noir.

CASTLE BALLROOM
RICHMOND
FRIDAY, SEPT. 1949
The Thames Valley Club
An "EASTBOURNE HOLIDAY"
DANCE
7·45 p.m. to 11·45 p.m.

Eddie Butt presents The Adastrians
M.C.: "CHAS" ARMSTRONG

LOOK!
★ HOLIDAY GIRL'S BATHING BEAUTY COMPETITION
★ "MISS THAMES VALLEY OF 1949"
★ AMATEUR RUMBA COMPETITION

TICKETS 3·6.
AND AT THE DOOR.

How many times do you visit an eatery and wish that you could import their décor to your home? Old graphics and vintage lighting play a huge part in Modern Rustic, and also provide both humour and personality in a scheme. The walls on this page are painted in Zinc. Opposite, bottom right, is a stunning antique cupboard that has been painted in Sel de Mer and aged gently with brown wax – the rustic frame is ragged with Sel de Mer and the wall panels are stunning, one-colour aged in Noir.

INDUSTRIAL CHIC MEETS PURE VINTAGE.

A TREAT

This clever image shows how lovely the simplicity of single [stem]s in antique bottles [can] be. The lighting is from Holland and [som]ething we introduced [to] the Attic duo a few [year]s ago. Obviously, we [all] share their love [of] French brocante, [oppo]site, which is the [c]ornerstone of our [o]wn reproduction collection.

ALL IN THE DETAIL

HAVE FAITH
IN YOURSELF
AND IN TH

YOU CAN RARELY SEE WHAT IS RIGHT IN FRONT OF YOU

As with so much in life,
it's all in the mix
and all about the detail.
Here's the bit where your
personal selection is what counts.
How you put it all together.
If you stick to your soul
and be true to yourself, you
cannot go wrong. We call it 'learning to
see...' and it's a mantra we've stuck to
for over 30 years.
To our minds, white china,
white linens, simple glassware,
beautiful old mirrors, plus a touch of
vintage industrial, is a heady cocktail that
is simply irresistible.
The result is sublime.

PAINTED COUNTRY

BACK TO BASICS

In many ways this chapter is probably the most important in the whole book. Painting, ageing and distressing furniture is really the main reason why our paint ever saw the light of day – we built our career on it and it is a decorating technique made in heaven.

Over the next 60 pages or so, we'll take you on a journey of discovery that will provide you with a whole gamut of techniques and skills that will last a lifetime – from the classic **one-colour ageing** to a surprising use of a household item that will age new wood beautifully. By the way, simple one-colour ageing was our most popular 'finish' back in the day, and has most certainly stood the test of time.

Indeed, if we succeed in our mission, you will be so liberated and excited by your new–found skills that you will most likely bore for England on the subject, (just like we do...) and just like many satisfied customers did after attending one of our courses, if history is anything to go by.

Along the way we'll also look at **two–colour ageing**, the French inspired look in which you see a painted base coat appearing randomly under the top coat, hinting at a previous life from times gone by. Then we'll look at a few other methods to achieve some fairly radical (by our standards) painted 'looks' on furniture, before discussing how to finish off your painted pieces so that they will last and last...

There are two projects in this chapter that, once tackled, should give you the confidence to create a whole manner of similar items, where the only limits will be that of your imagination – and a quick trawl on Pinterest will surely soon cure any creative blocks.

Above all, what we illustrate is born out of many years of producing and selling painted furniture – the core methods we use will allow you to achieve a professional result each and every time.

NOTHING EXCITES US MORE THAN WHEN WE
RECREATE SOMETHING THAT LOOKS SO AUTHENTIC.

ATTENTION. THE FOLLOWING PAGE CONTAINS NAKED IMAGES - SOME VIEWERS MIGHT FIND THIS DISTRESSING...

IT CALLS FOR A LOT OF IMAGINATION WHEN YOU'RE
CONFRONTED WITH FURNITURE IN THE RAW...

IN THE RAW

Well... we did warn you that you might find this image distressing - if you'll pardon the intentional pun. Naked furniture does take quite a bit of getting used to and even to the experienced eye, it can be hard to imagine the finished product, when it is so radically different. When purchasing furniture in this condition, you will often find that all the fixtures and fittings come separately, for ease of painting.

We do hope that this will not deter you though. Bespoke and brilliant transformations are at your fingertips and we will guide you every step of the way.

So, for example, these pieces here will first need to be stained with our water-based stain. This is to make the piece look realistic when you distress it. Then, very importantly, you need to apply two coats of shellac. This seals in the stain and also any knots at the same time - it is quick drying, so this shouldn't take to long to achieve. Then, you are ready to paint.

Back in the day, we always offered a 'natural' option on our furniture range and even today, with the launch of the wonderful new Signature collection in January 2016, customers have the ability to purchase most pieces naked, so that they have the choice of painting the piece themselves, in any one of the 33 colours.

More details of the Signature collection can be found on our website **www.grandillusions.co.uk**

THE ART OF PREPARATION

You won't want to hear this but we'll say it anyhow... Upcycling, or possibly painting furniture in general, is not exactly what you'd call a 'pure science'. It can be very easy and straightforward yet, for absolutely no apparent reason, sometimes, just sometimes, a small unforeseen problem might occur – completely at random, with no real rhyme nor reason. At Grand Illusions, we try to teach prevention rather than cure, although for the reasons stated above, it is wise to know both.

There is a view that chalk paint (in the generic sense) has probably been mis-sold throughout the world due to the sensational claims that you can literally '*slap it on anything...*'. We do agree, mostly, with this sentiment, but suggest that this was probably due more to the thirst for headlines and grand theatre in TV world, rather than any outlandish claims by a manufacturer – although this does seem to be getting a little out of hand.

As you will see in the next few pages, you can indeed apply our paint straight from the can, without any preparation *in some cases*. The paint does have very good adhesion qualities which is why we say that it can self-prime – but the clue is surely in the *italics*.

There are five different likely scenarios as a starting place for your project – by identifying this correctly, you could save yourself a lot of hassle later on... And don't worry, none of the treatments we suggest are especially onerous or complicated.

Please don't misunderstand, we get your enthusiasm and realise that time for all of us is a luxury. Yet do learn from our mistakes – in our haste, we once painted a complete dresser in a colour similar to our current **Artichaut**, straight from the can, ignoring our own advice. Within a few weeks, we had a pale green dresser covered in black polka dots, as we hadn't sealed in the knots. Despite what you may have heard, the art of preparation is not dead yet.

shellac for sealing in any nasty stains or knots...

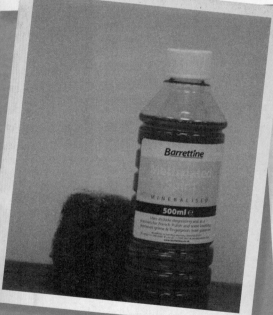

water-based woodstain

meths & wire-wool for de-waxing

medium grade sandpaper when you need a little light sanding

**THERE ARE FIVE DIFFERENT LIKELY SCENARIOS
WHEN PREPARING YOUR PIECE.
DON'T WORRY, IT'S ALL VERY EASY...**

ALREADY PAINTED.

So the piece you're going to upcycle is already painted and there are no visible signs of knots or stains coming through... This is the easiest scenario of them all, as you will see below — the hardest part will be selecting a new top colour.

It doesn't matter if you can see the brown wood exposed on the edges, this will only add to the charm when you two-colour age the piece later...

Step 1.
With the help of your sample boards and the opened tins of paint, choose which new colour the table is now going to become (fig.1).

Step 2.
Now give the piece a light sanding all over with a piece of medium-grade sandpaper (fig.2). This is just to take the shine off a little to help the paint adhere easily. This should take a few minutes nothing more...

Step 3.
Now you're ready to paint one or two coats of the new colour (fig.3). Don't spread the paint too thinly, it's meant to be like using double cream! We chose Nbr. 20 Fjord for a tonal result.

ALREADY VARNISHED...

In this case, the piece you've chosen is obviously
varnished. So, just like the painted piece opposite
normally all you have to do is give it a light sanding
and then start painting. Normally that is...

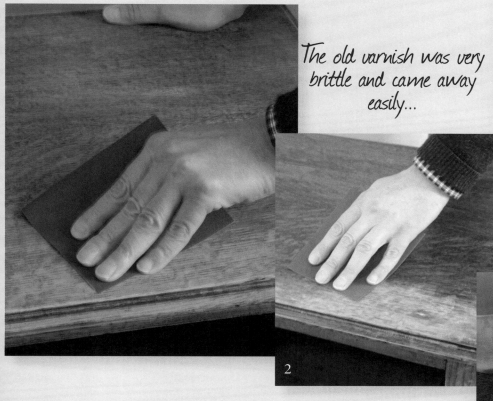

*The old varnish was very
brittle and came away
easily...*

*So to be 100% sure, we gave it one coat
of shellac as a sealant, just in case...*

Step 1.
This piece came from the local charity
shop and is typical of the brown
furniture you can find to upcycle.

Step 2.
We removed the knobs to make the job
easier. Usually all this would require
would be a light sanding prior to
painting (fig.1). As you can see, the top
coat of varnish just disappeared (fig.2),
so to be sure, we applied one coat of
shellac (fig.3). When dry, you can give
the shellac a very light sanding, to help
the paint adhere nicely.

Step 3.
Now you're ready to apply one or two coats
of the paint. We chose Nbr. 5 Earl Grey
with the top contrasting in Nbr 27 Noir.

PREVIOUSLY WAXED...

At the risk of sounding difficult, this is where our opinion differs from others out there. If your piece of furniture is waxed then you need to remove it before you paint. It's not rocket science - lovely water-based chalky paint meets oily, greasy wax - does that sound like a good marriage? To be precise, the paint would indeed stick, it just wouldn't stick around for very long - that's why some people also use wax as a resist between two colours. Now, you cannot have it both ways... Don't worry, de-waxing is really easy, as you can see below.

Use meths or sugar soap to take the wax off. It comes off easily...

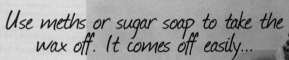

Keep shellac away from water and always clean brushes in methylated spirit

Step 1.
To remove the wax you will need either some methylated spirits or sugar soap and some medium grade wire wool (fig.1).

Step 2.
Gently rub in the direction of the grain with the meths and wire wool to remove the wax, then wipe clean with a damp soft cloth (fig.2). As you can see, the wax comes off easily. Allow to dry completely.

Step 3.
Next you need to seal the wood with one or two coats of shellac. When this is dry. you are now ready to paint (fig.3).

IN THE RAW...

So you've bought a piece of furniture 'in the raw'. To ensure 100% success, you need to do a couple of things before you start to paint. First, you need to stain the timber so it looks aged and then you need to seal in the stain (and any knots by the same process).

The furniture industry have been using water-based woodstains for years, now with the arrival of our Simply Stain it is available on the high street for the first time...

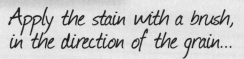

Apply the stain with a brush, in the direction of the grain...

Step 1.
Apply the water-based stain with a brush, moving in the direction of the grain where possible (fig.1). Allow to dry completely.

Step 2.
Seal in the stain with two coats of shellac (fig.2). Don't forget to clean your brushes with Meths rather than in water.

Step 3.
Shellac is very quick to dry. Once it has done so, you are ready to paint.

UNKNOWN ORIGIN...

Now here's the thing... sometimes you simply don't know
whether a piece has been varnished or sealed or not. We
call this 'wood of an unknown origin'. In these cases,
you need to seal the piece first as a precaution.

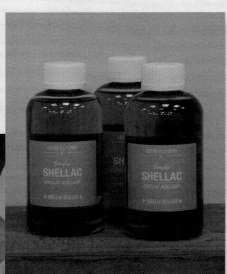

*After two coats of shellac, you can give the
piece a very light sanding to help the paint
adhere easily — this is not essential though...*

Step 1.
Apply the first coat of shellac and
allow to dry which should take no more
than 30 minutes (fig.1).

Step 2.
Next, apply a second coat of shellac.
We suggest two coats — as it dries so
fast, it's easy to miss an area the
first time around.

Step 3.
Now you're ready to paint one or two
coats of the new colour (fig.2). We
chose our new limited edition colour
Nbr 28 Menthe (fig.2).

ALREADY PAINTED	ALREADY VARNISHED	PREVIOUSLY WAXED	IN THE RAW	UNKNOWN ORIGIN
LIGHT SANDING	LIGHT SANDING	DE-WAX WITH METHS	STAIN	
		SHELLAC	SHELLAC	SHELLAC

NOW YOU'RE READY TO PAINT!

SO LET'S GET PAINTING...

Actually, we could have made the title here 'so let's get real...', as this is where we dispel some of the myths that surround the world of chalk paint. We know... we know... you're keen as mustard to start. But's let's just have a little chat first, so you know exactly what to expect. 'Warts an' all' honesty is always a good place to start in any new relationship.

Although we are obviously a little biased, we can really only talk about our paint here. There are, of course, other brands of chalk or milk paint available and, in many ways, they should perform similarly to ours. It is fair to say, though, that some contain additives and some are just a little different – it's as simple as that. Just for the record, the terms 'chalk paint' and 'milk paint' are generic for this type of truly historical paint and as such they cannot be trademarked, no matter what you might be led to believe.

Our paint is deliberately made to a consistency similar to that of double cream. Some colours vary in thickness, and this is due to the differing levels of natural pigments used to make a particular shade. If you want to make the paint even thicker, simply leave it overnight with the lid off. The idea is to use it straight from the can – there's no need to dilute it with water, although of course you might want to for some techniques as we'll show you later on.

Interestingly, people do have their own individual styles when it comes to painting. Some are cautious and very methodic, spreading the paint thinly as far as it will go. Whilst others are more carefree and generous. To be honest, we err towards the latter, as it is designed to be painted evenly but freely. It will dry very flat and it is very forgiving when it comes to technique. You can work quickly, you can use a roller or you could even spray it on, although this would require some dilution. This advice is not an invitation to just 'slap it on...' though. In life you tend to get back what you give. In our experience, taking a little care will get the very best result. Enjoy!

44

ALWAYS TAKE SOME TIME TO CREATE SAMPLE BOARDS SO YOU
CAN AVOID HAVING TO REPAINT OVER YOUR DISAPPOINTMENT LATER...

ONE–COLOUR AGEING

As previously stated, this is one of the all-time classics, the charm of which is unlikely to disappear anytime soon. By gently distressing your painted furniture, the appearance is softened and yet given depth and definition – once discovered, you'll never like plain again. But beware... it is a finish that can be much abused. Without a doubt, never have the immortal words **'less is more'** been more appropriate.

In the real world, so to speak, a piece of furniture will, in all likelihood, become scuffed and worn on the edges, on the corners, on the feet or around the knobs. It's pretty obvious really... so therefore your attempts to create a faded past should echo real life and rather handily, these are the easiest bits to sand back and reveal. The other key to achieving a highly believable and authentic result, is to 'age' the piece randomly – all too easily, you can find yourself distressing in a marvellously, yet inappropriate, symmetrical fashion.

Now speaking of ageing... it is our heartfelt belief that you're never too old to learn new tricks and during the creative process of producing this book, we have learned several. One of these enlightening moments occurred right at the start of our relaunch, when during one of our paint courses, a stockist mentioned that they use the humble **baby wipe** in addition to sandpaper to distress their furniture. It was a complete revelation and we've been hooked ever since – used in moderation, it removes the dried paint easily and leaves an appealing patina behind.

The other most important factor, as we explained when we extolled the virtues of preparation before, is that, when using new wood, it is vital to take the time and effort to stain and shellac before you paint. The reason is simple. Here we are, lovingly recreating a faded past, and nothing would give the game away more quickly than to see bright white wood shining through from beneath.

NEVER HAVE THE IMMORTAL WORDS
'LESS IS MORE' BEEN MORE APPROPRIATE.

ONE-COLOUR AGED...

So, as you'll have noticed from before, we have already given this piece a light sanding and a coat of shellac. Now we are going to give the main body two coats of Nbr 5 Earl Grey and when that's dry, paint the top of the chest in a contrasting Nbr 27 Noir. Then we'll gently age it with sandpaper and a cleansing wipe.

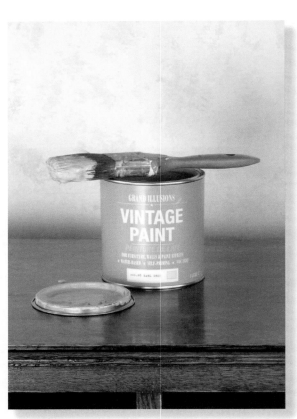

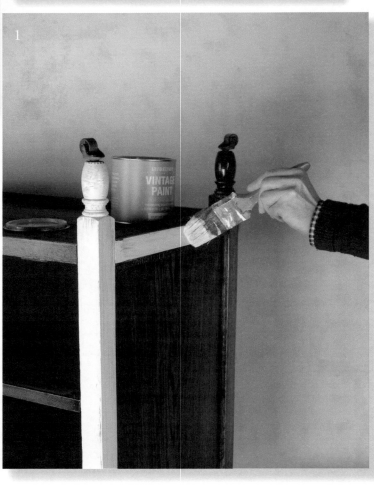

Step 1.
Remove the knobs and all the drawers to paint separately and make things easier. We turned the piece upside down too (fig.1).

Step 2.
Now paint the base with two coats of Earl Grey and, when dry, paint the top with two coats of Noir. Allow to dry completely.

Step 3.
Give all the surfaces a wipe with a dry kitchen scourer, to flatten the paint, if necessary. Then, with some medium grade sandpaper gently start the ageing process by sanding back the edges, the corners, the feet, the knobs — anywhere where natural wear and tear would occur (fig.2). Use a baby wipe for added distressing (fig.3). Use a clean cloth to wipe all the paint dust off.

Step 4.
Now you have to choose how to finish
off the piece with wax or our acrylic
flat varnish — we chose the latter. See
the next chapter for further guidance
on this.

SWEDISH–STYLE BROCANTE ADDS
A SOPHISTICATED FLOURISH TO
OUR UPCYCLED CHEST OF DRAWERS.

PROJECT: FRENCH SHELF

THE FRENCH SHELF PROJECT:
We've always taken the attitude that with patience and guidance, most people can make simple furniture. During the research for this book, we came upon a shelf just like this and thought we'd like to make one of our own. Here's how we did it...

Download the template from our website and use it to cut the shelf brackets.

1

2

3

Use a glass to mark the shape of the corners.

WHAT YOU'LL NEED...
2 x 18mm-thick pine furniture shelves,
one 1150 x 200mm, the other 850 x 200mm.
15 x 45mm batton - 1 piece cut to 1150mm
and 2 cut to 390mm in length.
40mm size 4 screws.
G clamp, electric drill/screwdriver, saw
and jig saw, medium grade sandpaper

First, fix the long batten to the two brackets as shown.

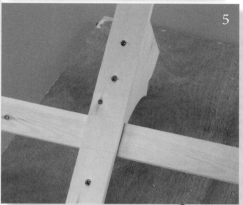

On each upright batten, drill three small pilot holes.

Step 1.
Cut the smaller (850 x 20mm)shelf into
2 x 300mm pieces, one from each end.
Then use the template to create the
shape of the brackets and carefully cut
out, using the jig saw (fig.1).

Step 2.
Drill pilot holes in the long batten
200mm in from each end. On the shorter
battens drill them at 40mm, 200mm and
330mm intervals from the top (fig.2).

Step 3.
On the larger shelf, use the jig saw
to cut the round corners, then use the
sandpaper to sand all the edges making
them as irregular as possible (fig.3).

Step 4.
Now assemble the shelf by fixing the
long batten to the shelf brackets with
the screws (fig.4). Then secure the
upright battens to the brackets
(fig.5). Finally, fix the top shelf to
the brackets by carefully drilling a
pilot hole and screwing in place.

We then stained and shellac'd the shelf before one-colour ageing in Nbr 6 Shutter Grey.

THESE ARE A FEW OF OUR FAVOURITE RECIPES:
VANILLE OVER MAROC,
SHUTTER OVER GOTLAND,
EARL GREY OVER NORDIC BLUE.

TWO–COLOUR AGEING

Two–colour ageing is where another paint colour is randomly revealed to suggest age, instead of the natural brown wood showing through. We've always thought of it as a vaguely French kind of a thing – certainly it is very popular in Europe when you buy painted furniture.

Back in the day, we had one colour combination that outsold all the others by about tenfold. That was Antique White over Stone, which today would be similar to a topcoat of **Sel de Mer** and a base colour of **Chapel**. These two colours work so well together it is not at all surprising to see how popular they are.

Other tried and tested successful pairings include: **Shutter** over a base of our new colour **Gotland** which is very traditional, **Vanille** or **Linen** over a very earthy **Maroc**, **Earl Grey** over the stunningly beautiful **Nordic Blue** or even working in a completely Grey palette, try **Earl Grey** or **Shutter** over the handsomely dark **Fossil** or vice versa. It is probably more usual, but by no means essential, to have the darker or stronger colour as the base and working tonally can be very successful too.

Tedious though this will sound, it is always wise to test your proposed colour combination on a sample board – rather spend a little time experimenting now, than waste time later repainting over a colour combination you're not happy with.

As before, we would urge restraint in your distressing – concentrate on the areas where you believe natural wear and tear would occur. And whilst we understand the urge to reveal the base colour after all this hard work, moments of madness where the patches revealed resemble a shoal of fish rather than gracefully fading areas, merely render the piece less believable. As the examples clearly show, a hint of the past is more than enough.

TWO-COLOUR AGED...

We wanted to give this reproduction bench a bit of
depth yet keep a grey colour scheme. So we decided to
two-colour age it in our palest shade, Earl Grey.
Working tonally can be just as successful
as a contrast of light and dark colours.

Step 1.
As this piece is already painted, all we had to
do was apply a coat of the varnish between the
base colour and the new top coat (fig.1). This is
merely to protect the base colour when you start
to distress the piece later.

Step 2.
When the varnish has dried, simply paint on two
coats of the top colour which in this case is
Nbr. 6 Earl Grey. Allow to dry.

Step 3.
Use a combination of sandpaper and baby wipes to
reveal the base colour, keeping in mind our
comments on realism (fig.2). We finished the
project with one more coat of Simply Varnish.

*If you were starting from scratch, you'd
apply two coats of the base colour, then
varnish and finish with two coats
of the top colour.*

Remember to distress randomly with sandpaper and baby wipes concentrating on all the places where natural wear & tear would occur.

SEL DE MER OVER SHUTTER GREY IS A
PERFECT COMBINATION. SANDING BACK RANDOMLY,
GIVES AN AIR OF AUTHENTICITY.

CREATING A RESIST

Over the next few pages we are about to enter a slightly more radical territory, a place where the genteel world of one- and two-colour ageing simply isn't enough...

So, you radicals, this is where we show you how to achieve a more dramatic look, one where rather more areas of distress are exposed – an effect that resembles heavily peeled paint, as you can see clearly on the table leg opposite. As ever, it is a technique that benefits from a modicum of restraint, as you still want to preserve an air of authenticity. Take a close look at genuine old battered pieces and try to emulate their design.

What we are talking about here is using a 'resist' – a substance, of some description, that will prevent the paint from sticking, so that it can be removed easily. In days gone by people would suggest (ourselves included) using a wax candle, rubbed randomly on the edges of furniture to provide such a medium. Some of us went on to discover that oily waxy patches and beautiful soft milk paint were not the perfect pairing – and when the piece came into contact with light and heat, said waxy patches that had not been thoroughly removed, had a nasty habit of reappearing just when you didn't want them to. After all, unless you're a genius with a photographic memory, how can you remember exactly where you placed the candle wax. Time to move on we feel...

Anyhow... in a book that is rapidly becoming an ode to household products, the solution we use to create a resist is **Copydex**. This glue seems to be a cross between PVA and a rubber solution and is unique. Artists' masking fluid would work in the same way. The beauty of the glue, however, is that when purchased in a bottle (as opposed to the tube variety), the accompanying brush is the perfect device to 'splodge' the glue on randomly – no artistic experience required.

A RUBBER SOLUTION

IN A BOOK THAT IS RAPIDLY BECOMING AN ODE TO
HOUSEHOLD PRODUCTS, THE SOLUTION WE USE
TO CREATE A RESIST IS COPYDEX.

CREATING A RESIST...

Sometimes a bit of mega-distressing is called for, so here's our way of achieving this. This is, no doubt, an acquired taste but it can save time on a large project and the Copydex does produce a deliciously random result.

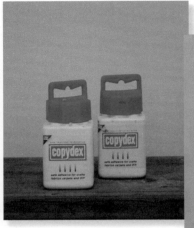

Splodging on the glue...

Surely best

Step 1.
You need to use the Copydex as a barrier between, in this case, the stained and shellac'd wood of the table. You can use it between colours too, as we did on the wall opposite.

Step 2.
Using the brush from the tub, literally 'splodge' the glue on randomly where you want the ageing to occur (fig.1). Allow to dry, at which point it will be transparent.

Step 3.
Now apply two coats of paint — for this we used Nbr 9 Chapel. And then, when dry, distress in the normal way with sandpaper — this will reveal the transparent patches which you peel off as shown (fig.2). What fun!

Step 4.
Clean with a dry cloth and then use Simply Varnish to finish the task (fig.3).

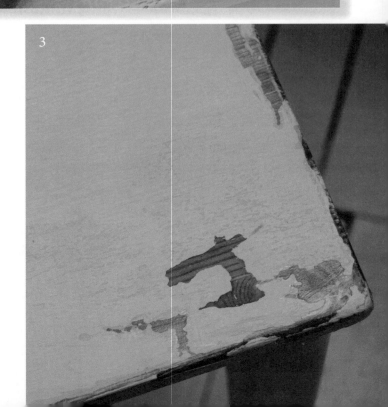

FOR A WALL PROJECT
LIKE THIS YOU CREATE
IRREGULAR—SHAPED
PATCHES WITH THE
GLUE THEN CAREFULLY
PAINT INSIDE THEM.

THE TRANSLUCENT LAYERS OF PAINT
GIVE DEFINITION AND DEPTH TO THE FINISH.

WASH AND RAG

Colourwashing is of course a term used normally in association with wall treatments rather than furniture, yet the translucent layers employed certainly add a kind of depth and definition to the finished work – especially when heavily sanded-back to reveal the wood beneath.

And surprisingly it works particularly well on smooth surfaces like MDF. Indeed our first inspiration for this technique came from a French furniture manufacturer called Henri Quinta – he produced stunning beautifully plain shaker-like pieces of furniture, very flat wood with straight edges (hence the similarity to MDF) and these would be painted in bright colours, heavily distressed to reveal the wood – pure theatre and highly desirable. You can still see examples of his work on the internet.

The key to successful colourwashing is getting the tones right. In the example here, we added fifty per cent **Sel de Mer** to **Verdigris** to create a colour for the starting point, the base coat, which you paint on as normal. We then created two or three 'washes' which is the main colour (in this case Verdigris) mixed and diluted with variable amounts of water – start with the weakest and build up the layers, using the strongest solution, the one with the least water added, as the final top coat. Paint these washes on randomly, allowing the lower levels to shine through and use a rag to blend in…

As you will see, another similar technique which is simplicity itself, is simply to 'rag' on the paint randomly, leaving patches of wood exposed. You really couldn't get a quicker or more 'instant' result.

Whilst undoubtedly these techniques are a bit of an acquired taste, they do work well in the right location – we particularly liked them in our Cabin Fever story on page 100.

WASHING...

Colourwashing is more usually associated with walls rather than furniture, yet the same translucent appeal works here too giving depth and definition. The secret of success is getting the tones correct and blending them in successfully.

Step 1.
The idea is to start pale and build up the colour layer by layer. So we painted the body and drawers with two coats of a mix made up of 50% Sel de Mer and Verdigris.

Step 2.
Create three 'washes' by mixing water into the Verdigris paint. Try 3 parts water to one part paint as your weakest one, then 2 parts water to paint and finally 1 part of each. Starting with the weakest solution, brush on each wash loosely a small area at a time blending in with a clean cloth (fig.1). You might have to experiment a little to find the ideal mix.

Step 3.
When completely dry, heavily distress using a baby wipe (fig.2). Finish with a coat of Simply Varnish rather than the wax, as this might take more of the wash off.

You might have to experiment to get the consistency of the 'washes' to your liking. Just make sure the last one is strong enough to make a difference...

Take the handles off to make it easier to
apply the layers of washes...

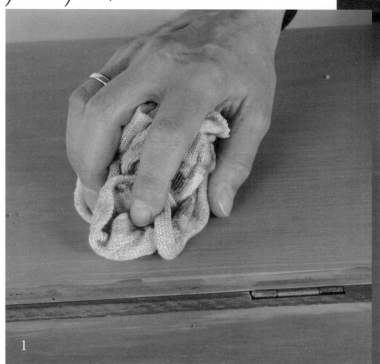

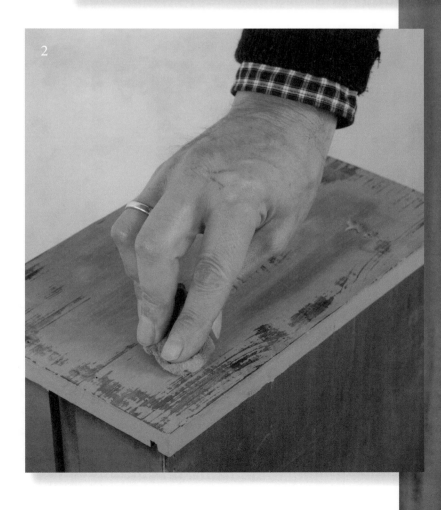

RAGGING...

Ragging is used when you need to get some paint on in a hurry and you don't mind a highly distressed appearance. It's about as simple as it can get and has a great appeal – all very coastal don't you think?

You literally wipe the paint on with a cloth, leaving areas unpainted as you see fit. This table would have looked great daubed in Sel de Mer as well. Then you take it back with wire wool.

Step 1.
Just get a clean cloth and 'daub' the paint on randomly, leaving areas wildly exposed (fig.1). Repeat on all four sides and on the inside legs too. Leave to dry.

Step 2.
Now take it back even further using wire wool (fig.2) – this will help it to blend in and look more realistic.

Step 3.
Finally, varnish or wax as you see fit.

DRY BRUSHING

In this picture you can actually see two techniques we have already covered earlier clearly in evidence. We have ragged the old door at the back and we have used Copydex to create the peeling paint/distressed effect, as part of two–colour ageing the furniture. We hope you agree they look very effective in this story.

This piece of furniture is called a Farinier, the design of which is based on a very traditional larder cupboard from France, which is part of our Signature collection launched in January 2016. Onto this, we have also dry brushed a random coat of **Earl Grey** on top of the **Sel de Mer** to give a very old and loveworn appearance. These two colours work very well together, especially in this context.

Dry brushing says what it does on the can, so to speak... It's just a vaguely fancy name for applying the paint with a brush, having wiped off much of the excess paint beforehand – by being dry it gives you a random coating, rather than a normal solid layer. We've then blended it in with a cloth and sanded it back almost immediately. Finish with a coat of Simply Varnish.

A little like the ragging on the previous page, dry brushing is a quick way to get a second colour in place, providing you want the heavily distressed look. It is a useful technique to master, especially when it comes to painted floors, because when you're creating a look-a-like limewashed floor, dry brushing is the way you'd do it.

EARL GREY DRY BRUSHED OVER SEL DE MER
GIVES THE PIECE A LOVEWORN CHARM.

To start, we used Copydex to create
resist & then painted it Sel de M

Use a pad or board of
some sort to wipe off the
excess paint.

1

DRY BRUSHING

Dry Brushing literally means what it says — getting
all the excess paint off the brush so only the vaguest
residue transfers onto the furniture, floor or wall. It
is a bit like the Ragging you saw just before, you just
need to be confident and go for it...

*Use a clean cloth to blend
in the brush marks.*

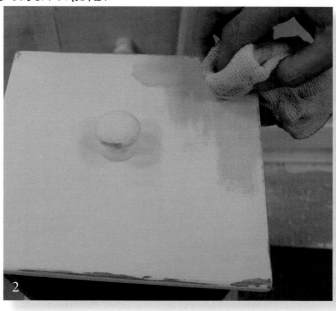

*Sand back immediately to
blend in further.*

Step 1.
Dip your brush into the Earl Grey paint
and wipe off any excess on a board or
pad you've created (fig.1).

Step 2.
Working a small area at a time, paint
sparingly onto the furniture, spreading
and blending in with a cloth (fig.2).

Step 3.
Sand back immediately to further blend
in the dry brushing (fig. 3).

Step 4.
A coat of varnish to finish would be
the preferred option, to avoid losing
any of the delicate dry brushing.

*Earl Grey works so well
over Sel de Mer !*

AND SO TO FINISH...

Now this is where our history and experience differs from all the other so-called chalk or milk paint producers. We believe it's fair to say that we were the only company to use this kind of paint to produce hand-painted furniture on a commercial basis, resulting in literally hundreds and hundreds of pieces being sold and delivered every year.

With that in mind, it was absolutely imperative that the piece had to arrive with the customer, possibly many hundreds of miles away, in the showroom–condition it left us. As a consequence, our opinion on 'finishing off' is a little different - our preference each and every time would be to use a flat acrylic varnish, especially when it's like the new improved formula 'Simply Varnish' being launched at the same time as this book. Wax, which can mark easily and, with its intolerance to water, would just be too volatile.

Waxing, though, is of course very traditional. And, undeniably, there are times when the richness and intensity achieved is highly desirable. But on a large piece like a dresser, this can be hard work and some people are a little disappointed when working in the paler tones, to lose the subtle and delicate nature of the paint shade.

As we mentioned, our new formula for 'Simply Varnish' is much improved. It hardly changes the colour at all, even on the palest of tones, and ironically, to a degree, has the silky feel of wax - yet it provides a durable, water– and heat–resistant film. One coat should be sufficient for most tasks. It is easy to apply and, of course, the brushes simply wash out in water. This new varnish has been under discussion for some time and we are absolutely delighted to finally bring this to market. Other acrylic varnishes are of course available, but we are confident we are working with the best now...

Wax or varnish... the choice is yours...

FLAT VARNISH OR WAX LYRICAL?

SWEDISH OR GREEK? THE LEFT HAND SIDE WAS VARNISHED
AND THE RIGHT WAS WAXED. INTERESTINGLY, ON THIS OCCASION
YOU CAN HARDLY TELL THE DIFFERENCE...

FLAT VARNISH...

We make no secret of the fact that we prefer to finish a piece with our acrylic Simply Varnish. With the
new improved formula, it's easier to use, flatter
(you witness hardly any colour change at all) and
Eco-friendly — you can wash the brushes in water —
what's not to like ?

some of the ageing occurred when we removed the masking tape. Love it!

Hardly any change in colour...

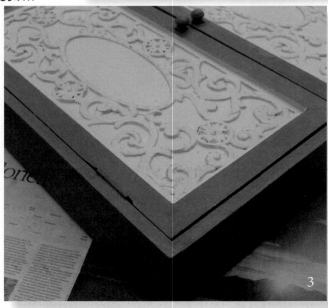

Don't pour out too much at a time and always mix thoroughly before use

Step 1.
Having shaken or stirred the varnish to
mix thoroughly, pour a sufficient amount
into a bowl (fig.1).

Step 2.
Brush on sparingly and evenly then
brush out any runs or drips (fig.2).
It will be slightly luminous to start
with...

Step 3.
As you will see, it dries quickly to a
flat finish, hardly changing the colour
at all and giving you a wipeable
surface (fig.3). Apply a second coat if
you feel it necessary.

Step 4.
For hard-wearing areas like kitchen
tables, apply one or two coats of a
satin acrylic varnish first and then
flatten with one or two coats of the
new formula Simply Varnish.

OR WAX?

Our own personal preferences aside, there is no doubt that wax
provides a rich and intense depth to the finished piece.
As a consequence, it will change the colour, not that this is
necessarily a negative. Just avoid using it on tabletops for example,
as it can easily mark when in contact with moisture.

Always wear gloves when using wax !

*As you can see,
wax will intensify
the colour a little...*

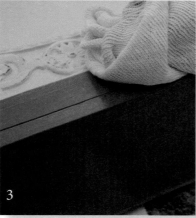

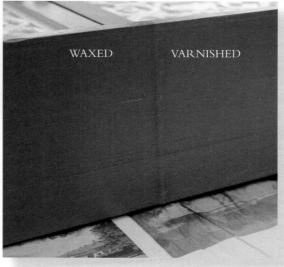

WAXED   VARNISHED

Step 1.
You will need a soft cloth or brush to
apply the wax (fig.1). Do keep the area
well ventilated, as even our milder
waxes have a strong aroma.

Step 2.
Apply quickly and sparingly, making
sure that you have created an even
coating (fig.2). You can tell where
you've applied the wax, as it will be
slightly darker in appearance.

Step 3.
Leave overnight to harden and cure
completely. Then take a completely new
soft cloth and buff to a sheen (fig.3).

*Glossy or matt ? You choose...
It really does depend on the
project in hand.*

IT TAKES A
LOT OF
COURAGE TO
COVER YOUR
NEWLY CREATED
PIECE IN
A DARK BROWN
WAX

BROWN WAX

Just when you thought you had the hang of it all, along comes another possibility. And once again, it's probably the French we have to thank for this treatment.

Simply Brown Wax is used a little differently to that of Simply Clear Wax. In our painterly world we use it to 'antique' a piece of furniture to simulate age – yet of course it was first invented to enrich and stain white natural wood.

As you will see, working a small area at a time, it is wise to first apply a coat of the clear wax – follow this with a coat of the brown wax, working in to all the nooks and crannies, the architrave and so on, as shown. Then you remove the excess brown wax with more clear wax, leaving a suitable residue behind – working and nurturing the area until you're happy with the amount of brown patina remaining. The purpose of the original coat of clear wax is to give you more time to 'work' the area, as the wax can dry and harden quite quickly.

You should then leave it overnight and polish up to a sheen if required. Some people prefer the matt look, in which case, simply leave the wax to dry and harden.

This technique is also used with Craquelure Varnish to great effect as you will see on Page 138. A possible alternative would be to use an acrylic artists' colour like Raw Umber, using it neat or with a little water, once again working it in to all the crevices. It takes a little practice, so best to try a sample board first.

USING BROWN WAX...

Although Brown Wax was originally created to lend richness and colour to natural wood, we use it, in our painterly world, for something quite different — making furniture look very shabby indeed. It's not for the faint-hearted by the way...

The clear wax is important as it gives you more time!

Step 1.
Apply a coat of clear wax to the panel you're working on (fig.1).

Step 2.
Now apply a coat of brown wax using a cloth or brush, working in to all the architrave and corners.

Step 3.
Then, with a clean cloth and more clear wax, remove the excess brown wax swiftly, leaving a suitable residue behind. The clear wax is used to give you a longer working time, as it stops the brown wax from drying.

Step 4.
Leave overnight and buff to a sheen if required (fig.3).

This might be a shock the first time you try it...

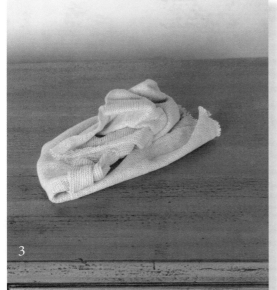

Some people prefer not to buff it up to a shine...

PASS THE VINAIGRE

In doing the research for this book we did stumble across some gems which we were, previously, blissfully unaware of and this is among the best. It's a fact that household vinegar is a brilliant medium with which to age natural wood - indeed, we'd go so far as to say it's quite astonishing. Who would ever have thought it?

The technique is very simple, if a little fragrant at times, but do persevere, as it is well worth it. The acidic solution produces a variety of patinas on different types of wood as it oxidises. It seems to love oak and goes very dark easily, but it is at its finest when employed on simple white pine or beech as it results in a lovely mellow colour.

According to our experiments, **Apple Cider Vinegar** seems to produce the best looking result for our taste. **Clear Malt Vinegar** works very well with a darker grey patina, but sometimes takes on a reddish hue, whilst **White Wine Vinegar** takes on a lighter appearance.

And this discovery makes achieving that much–coveted old wood appearance simple, easy and, above all, incredibly believable. This in turn translates into several more easy projects without too much thought. For example, as the next project illustrates rather beautifully, you can now make endless lengths of Shaker peg rails at a fraction of the price you'd pay in a shop - and they're far nicer too. Another idea would be to 'age' white plywood planks (see Simple Ply Floor on page 117) in the three types of vinegar and then use them as floorboards - the changing tones could look stunning.

Similarly, when combined with the skills you'll learn in the Image Transfer chapter, the possibilities are enormous. As ever though, before embarking on any large project, do experiment with some sample boards first, as results can be a little variable.

RESTORATION EXPERTS USE ACETIC ACID – THE MAIN INGREDIENT
IN VINEGAR - TO REFURBISH OLD TIMBER.

USING VINEGAR TO AGE WOOD

On this page we explain how you can experiment with vinegars to oxidize wood and create some very natural looking aged timbers. Use this newfound skill in harmony with the ideas in the Image Transfer chapter and the possibilities are endless...

Use the vinegars with plenty of ventilation, as they can be a little fragrant!

Step 1.
Get yourself three types of vinegar, clear Malt, White Wine and Apple Cider (fig.1).

Step 2.
As a rough guide, we put 125ml of each vinegar into a jar and a ball of wire wool approximately 50mm dia (fig.2). The bigger the wire wool, the stronger the solution will be. Now leave for 24 hours without covering.

Step 3.
When ready, use the wire wool in these solutions to apply the vinegar to the wood (fig.3). You should see a change almost immediately, but best to wait at least a further 24 hours to see how it has cured. The time taken does seem to depend on climate and it can take seven days to cure properly. Exposure to sunlight will aid the process.

Step 4.
Patience is a virtue – the wood on the right was aged with Apple Cider Vinegar and is just the result we were hoping for...

PROJECT: SHAKER PEG RAIL.

SHAKER PEG RAILS

The charm of the simple Shaker peg rail never ceases to be appealing. Now armed with this new technique, you can create endless lengths to your exact requirements. You can find the naked pegs easily on the internet — do seek out the ones with screw fittings, as they are much easier to work with.

Use an old box to secure the pegs whilst you stain them...

The rail on the far end was stained with our woodstain !

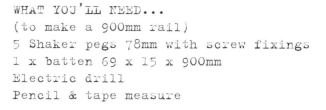

Step 1.
Age the timber and the pegs with vinegar as described previously (fig.1). Alternatively, just use our Simply Stain woodstain — the rail on the far right of the picture was created in this manner (fig.2).

Step 2.
Mark the position of the pegs every 150mm along the rail with a pencil (fig.3). Drill a small pilot hole for each peg (fig.4).

Step 3.
Now just simply screw in each peg (fig .5). Just how easy was that?

BLANK CANVAS

WALL TO WALL

One of the questions we're asked a lot is whether you can use our type of paint on walls. The answer is 'yes' and is it especially suited to areas where you need the wall to breathe – remember it doesn't have the plasticky vinyl that most emulsions have. As a consequence, though, we always point out a couple of things.

Unlike regular emulsion you cannot 'cut-in' at the top and bottom ('cutting in' is the process where you paint all the tricky bits first, like the top of the skirting or where the wall meets the ceiling – before you paint the bulk of the wall). The reason for this is, because the paint dries very quickly, the darker colours might be a little patchy where the two sections meet. It means you need to paint a whole area in one go. We're erring on the side of caution here, as we do know many people who say that this was not a problem for them. The other factor is that whilst stunningly flat, it is by it's nature very soft, so offers only a limited wipeable factor. This can be remedied by applying a coat of the new improved Simply Varnish, as this too dries very flat.

In this chapter, we explore some classic vintage wall treatments like two-tone or colourwashing and we also provide some ideas for using wood on walls that are 'de rigueur' right now... One of the best ideas to impart here is how, by simply cutting plywood into 200mm strips, you can emulate old floorboards which in turn, can be used as wonderful wall planking too. After all, wooden walls are not only attractive to look at, but also very practical too as they make fixing shelves, mirrors and pictures a doddle. Onwards and upwards...

PAINTING A WALL
IN TWO TONES
EPITOMISES
VINTAGE STYLE...

Experiment with your colours using sample pots or boards before embarking on the walls...

TWO-TONE WALLS

To be fair, you do not need to use our type of paint to create a two-tone wall, regular emulsion would work perfectly fine — just maybe not as chalky, flat and matt. The technique would be just the same.

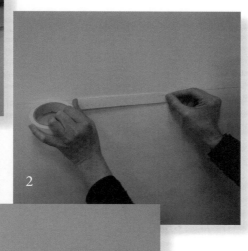

Use a low tack masking tape if you can get it...

Step 1.
Using a spirit level, draw a line in pencil across the wall where you want the two colours to meet (fig.1). Fix masking tape <u>under</u> the line, as you'll be painting the lighter colour first (fig.2).

Step 2.
Paint two coats of the top colour (Vanille) onto the wall using a roller and, where necessary, a brush too (fig.3). Do ensure to come off the masking tape rather than paint towards it.

Step 3.
When completely dry, carefully remove the tape and, using new tape, reposition <u>above</u> the line (fig.4). Now apply two coats of the base colour (Nordic Blue). When dry, remove the tape again (fig.5).

TWO TONE
COLOUR SCHEMES
WORK
PARTICULARLY
WELL WITH
UNFITTED KITCHENS,
LIKE THIS ONE
WHICH WE
INTRODUCED TO
OUR COLLECTION
EARLIER THIS
YEAR.

CREATING WOODEN WALLS...

The hardest bit about creating wooden walls is the fact
that most of them need to be fixed onto battens.
The state of your existing walls will determine the
level of skill required to accomplish these ideas.

If you have a timber walls already, then you're
laughing, as you'd probably be able to nail or screw
directly into them. If you have a stone or brick wall,
then you'll need to use a masonry drill and wallplugs
to fix the battens.

Worst-case scenario is a stud wall. Here you will need
to purchase a meter that can identify where the studs
are (and any electric cables for that matter).
Once you know where the studs are, you can screw
straight into them if they're wood. If they're metal,
there are specialist screws available for this task.

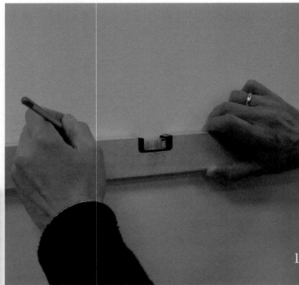

1

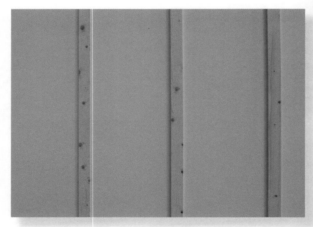

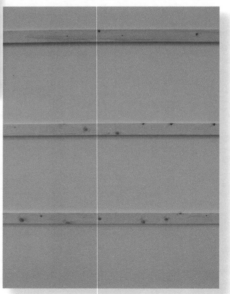

*Depending on the project,
battens will need to be fixed,
either horizontally or vertically.*

98

Use either 45 x 12mm or
45 x 18mm battens for this task.

The best idea ever...
use 12mm or 18mm plywood
cut into 200mm strips to make
brilliant floorboards or wall panels.

Step 1.
Use a spirit level to draw guidelines
as to where the battens should be
positioned on the wall (fig.1). We have
indicated the ideal distance between the
battens on each of the wall treatments.

Step 2.
Whichever type of wall you are fixing to,
it is always a good idea to pre-drill
guiding holes in the battens – use these
holes to mark on the wall where the
wallplugs are needed. If you're fixing to
a stud wall, make these holes correspond
to the location of the upright studs.

Step 3.
Fix the battens to the wall with either
wallplugs or screws, according to the
type of wall you have.

CABIN FEVER

Here is the first project to use plywood planks to help create wonderful and inexpensive wall panels. You can get the local timber yard or DIY store to cut them to a width of 200mm and a length to suit.
For walls we use 12mm thickness ply.

ragging in the wash...

before & after...

Step 1.
For this project, you need to fix the battens to the wall vertically before you start, at 450mm intervals. Depending on the width of your wall, make sure you fix a batten where any joins occur. The ply had a red tint, so we stained it with our woodstain first, to calm it down a little.

Step 2.
Now create a thin wash using roughly 50% Earl Grey paint to 50% water. Apply with a large brush and use a cloth to rag into the wooden plank (fig.1).

Step 3.
Now fix to the battens horizontally using panel pins and a hammer. As you lay each row, stagger the joins so that they don't all occur in one place.

LOVING THE COMBINATION OF COLOURS HERE.
FOSSIL, EARL GREY AND SHUTTER ALL MIX BEAUTIFULLY
WITH THE NATURAL WOOD, RUST AND ZINC ELEMENTS.

NEW ENGLAND GREY

This scheme uses exactly the same technique as
Cabin Fever on the previous page, so no need for any
step-by-step instructions here. The only difference is
that, instead of staining and washing the planks,
you will need to shellac them first and then apply two
coats of paint – we used our new colour Fossil.
If you need them wipeable, then varnish to finish.

*the planking would be just perfect
for creating a backdrop to a verandah
or summerhouse.*

You could use any colour to paint the planks.
This dark grey Fossil is very rich and very of
the moment, although for a completely different
atmosphere, you could consider a paler
grey like Shutter or Zinc.
Painting them Sel de Mer would give a very
summerhouse or conservatory feel
to the end result.
The pale grey wooden floor is perfect for all
these options.

BATTEN & PEG RAIL

Here the simple batten is used to great effect to create a relief and detail on the wall. Combined with more of the Shaker peg rail, the result is a mix of contemporary and vintage style.

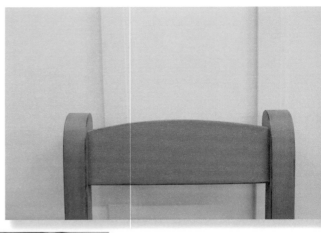

we used the thinner style battens for this project. ie. 12mm thick

Step 1.
For this project, unless you already have a timber wall, you will need to line the wall with sheets of 12mm ply, before you fix the vertical battens. To do this, you will need to fix the first lot of battens horizontally to the wall and nail the ply to these. This will make fixing the upright battens and peg rail so much easier.

Step 2
When the sheets of ply are safely in place, prime or seal any knots with primer or shellac. Do the same for the battens and then paint everything with at least two coats of Sel de Mer. NB: We used a 940mm plank of wood to create a simple skirting.

Step 3.
Fix the skirting in place with panel pins and then, using a spirit level, mark and fix the battens in place at 300mm intervals. Make sure that the positioning of the battens covers any joins in the plywood panels.

Step 4.
For the peg rail, fix pegs at 150mm intervals and then fix to the wall about 1.8m from the ground, using a spirit level. Note that the pegs should sit in line with the battens, and in the middle of the gaps.

SOMETIMES, SIMPLICITY IS THE KEY TO A GOOD DECISION...

if you were feeling fancy, you could add horizontal pieces as well, which would be very smart.

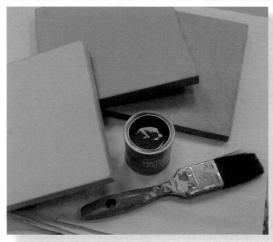

we left the pegs in their natural stained colour.

GREY PANEL WALL

This is a variation on a theme and similar in style and execution to the Batten & Peg Rail project shown previously. Here we've used the gorgeously warm tones of our Hurricane paint which goes very well with our simple plywood plank flooring.

Step 1.
Once again, you will need to line the wall with plywood sheeting as previously described, this time only going three-quarters up the wall. Instead of battens, use 1.8m lengths of 94 x 18mm wood, available at most DIY stores.

Step 2.
As before, use the planks for the skirting and also for the peg rail and shelf, which sits at the top of the upright panels. Paint everything in two coats of Hurricane, having primed or shellac'd as before. To make the panelling wipeable, you will need to apply one coat of Simply Varnish. When dry, fix the uprights at 450mm intervals.

Step 3.
On the top horizontal surface, with the depth of the original batten, the ply and these new panels, you should have sufficient depth to carefully affix a shelf.

Step 4.
Finally, screw in the pegs, again at 450mm intervals but in between the uprights.

THE CLASSIC T&G WALL...

Tongue & Groove must surely be one of the all-time decorating classics and yet it never seems to lose it's charm. In a way it was the inspiration behind all of our wall concepts and maybe, just maybe, the simple ply wall panels will be the successor. They are easier and cheaper to work with for sure.

The T&G you buy in most DIY stores is a little on the flimsy side and can lead to frustrations trying to fix the planks together. Proper timber merchants tend to sell what is called 'bead and butt' - this is a stronger version of T&G, which is easier to assemble, with a beading on each plank.

Painting T&G is not quite as easy as you'd think either, as you need to paint in all the grooves as well as on the flat surfaces - a mini roller will help, but you'll still need a brush to fill in the gaps where the roller did not quite reach. It's worth it though...

We've painted this wall in two coats of Sel de Mer, having first primed or shellac'd it to seal in the knots of the raw wood. Whilst white may be very traditional, T&G painted in a mid grey like Shutter, a dark grey like Fossil, or even a dark blue like Nordic Blue, would look very smart indeed.

Another idea would be to buy the T&G pre-cut in 1.8m lengths. This would enable you to create a three-quarters high panelling. Fix a small shelf across the top, carefully screwing down into the batten behind and then wallpaper the section above - this would give a distinctly contemporary twist to this everlasting vintage classic.

Like the other examples, the T&G needs to be fixed to horizontal battens as before.

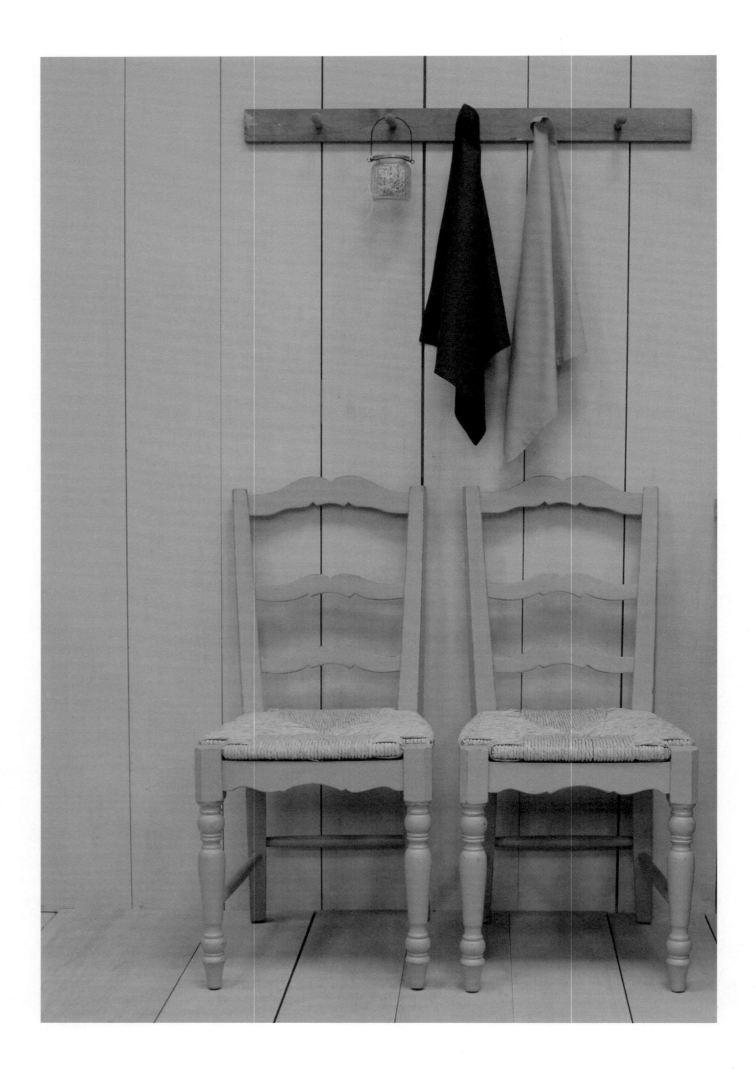

COASTAL PANELLING

This is a variation on the method we used to create the panelling in Cabin Fever and the New England Grey story. As we suggested, sheets of ply pre-cut into 200mm strips make wonderful panelling. Here they are given a distinctly coastal appearance.

if the boards are different colours, you need to add further coats of the wash until they match...

we used 12mm ply for this project.

the result needs to be fairly textured in appearance. You can always sand back a little if needed.

Step 1.
First of all, you will need to line the wall with horizontal battens.

Step 2.
Next, you need to create a fairly thick wash of Earl Grey diluted with 30% water (fig.1) — it needs to be strong enough to change the colour, yet allow the knots to show through a little.

Step 3.
Apply the wash with a large brush (fig.2), painting in the same direction along the length of the plank. Allow to dry completely.

Step 4.
Fix to the battens with panel pins, leaving a tiny gap between each plank.

THIS KIND OF SIMPLE PANELLING ON THE WALLS AND ON THE FLOOR
IS A REALLY EASY WAY OF ACHIEVING A COASTAL LOOK.

PIED A TERRE

GENTLY FLOORED

We touched on this in the previous chapter. One of the most exciting ideas in this entire book, is featured overleaf, yet at first glance you may not think it so... It was a light-bulb moment for us when we first read about it, especially as it solved a particular problem we had at home, something we'd been trying to find a solution for since the day we moved in, two years ago. Further research led us to realise that 'floating floors' are perfectly acceptable and also part of the plan.

Unfortunately, you see, upon arrival we found that our house was blessed with two whole floors boasting beyond-hideous ceramic tiles – let's just say circa 1970's swirly brown. The builder suggested more tiles, which allegedly looked like limed wood. To be fair, they sort of did look realistic. But then when the estimate had far too many noughts on for our liking, we thought 'Nah!'. It was time to think outside of the box – a random posting on Pinterest saved the day.

It transpires that if you cut plywood sheeting into 200mm strips, they can very easily start to resemble old floorboards. And, frankly, if you use the white pine variety, all you have to do is stain and varnish and you'll be amazed how realsitic they will look. The secret is in the width and the small gaps you leave in between the boards. In our case we fixed them to battens, laid on top of the tiles, but normally you simply fix to a first layer of plywood sheeting. The possibilities are are of course endless.

In this chapter we also explore some other floor treatments including the fabulous geometric faux tiles made from MDF that were inspired by an old floor we saw in Mallorca. There is, of course, the classic painted checked floor – still going strong in our painterly world – and for another quick fix, how about creating your own floorcloths?

GRAND ILLUSIONS
PAINT
VINTAGE

IN A HALLWAY, IN THE BACKSTREETS OF PALMA,
WE FOUND A TIMELESS, CLASSIC CERAMIC FLOOR.

THE POSSIBILITIES ARE ENDLESS FOR THIS INEXPENSIVE
AND HIGHLY ATTRACTIVE FLOORING CONCEPT.

SIMPLE PLY FLOOR

white plywood is easier for the task as it can simply be stained...

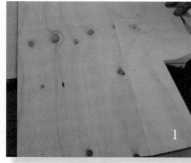

If you take nothing else from this book, do take this...
Using humble plywood to simulate old floors is such a great idea. The trick is to have the ply cut to 200mm wide strips and, because it does possess an element of texture, the boards are believable. You can simply stain and varnish, age with different vinegars, give a coastal look with a wash (see page 118) or simply just paint and varnish it.
And it is so inexpensive.

to tone down the reddish ply, we made a wash with 50% water, 50% Earl Grey paint.

when you lay the planks, you need to leave a 5mm gap where they meet the wall, to allow for expansion.

Step 1.
First get your local DIY store to cut the plywood sheets into 200mm strips. We used 18mm for added strength (fig.1).

Step 2.
How you start does depend on the type of floor you have already. For most scenarios it is likely that you'll need to line the floor first with sheets of 12mm ply. Ask your DIY store to cut them to size for you.

Step 3.
We had reddish ply, so had to tone it down with stain (fig.2)and then a very thin wash of Earl Grey paint, diluted with at least 50% water (fig 3). White ply would be easier to use, as you simply have to stain it first (fig.1).

Step 4.
Nail the floorboards to the ply sheeting, leaving a small gap between each for added realism. To finish, cover the floor with one coat of acrylic satin varnish, followed by a coat of our new improved Simply Varnish to flatten.

COASTAL WHITEWASHED FLOOR

This is another variation of the Simple Ply Floor (page 116). Here we took the same ply floorboards and washed them in a strong solution of Earl Grey paint mixed with water. By washing them, as opposed to painting them properly, you can achieve a slightly translucent result which resembles whitewashing or liming.

make a strong wash solution diluting the paint with around 30% water.

Step 1.
You can use either the reddish or white plywood for this treatment. Have the ply cut into strips at the DIY store as before.

Step 2.
You will now need to wash each floorboard with a fairly strong colourwash made up of Earl Grey paint, diluted with around 30% water (fig.1). Apply in such a way as to ensure elements of the base are barely visible (fig.2). By using a wash as opposed to solid paint, you should be able to see the knots and blemishes showing through (fig.3).

Step 3.
Lay the floor onto a 12mm plywood sheeting base (as before) and nail securely. Remember to leave a 5mm gap where the floor meets the wall, and also a small gap between planks for realism.

Step 4.
As this is a floor, you will now need to seal in your wash. Do this by applying one coat of acrylic satin varnish and leave to dry overnight. Then apply one coat of Simply Varnish to flatten it. Always test a small piece first.

use small nails to secure the boards to the plywood sheeting base. You could consider hiring or buying a nail gun to make the task easier...

FAUX SPANISH TILES

Here's an idea that we've updated from one of our previous books. It still has just as much charm as it did before. Using MDF squares to make tiles is an inexpensive option, warmer on bare feet and offers you the ability to bespoke your own design. Geometric-style tiles are very much in vogue right now. We spotted this pattern in an old apartment in Mallorca, and recreated our own version. We love it...

Zinsser is the strongest primer and stain repellant you can buy...

Step 1.
Assess how many tiles you need and get your local DIY store to cut a 2440 x 1220mm sheet of 9mm MDF into 290mm squares. This will give you 32 'tiles' per sheet (fig.1).

Step 2.
Now prime each tile with two coats of the shellac-based primer Zinsser. It is important that you prime the top and the sides of each square (fig.2).

Step 3.
Then, paint each one again with two coats of Earl Grey. We used a mini-roller to make things quicker and easier. As before, you need to paint the top and sides (fig.3).

Step 4.
Now you need to make yourself a stencil. We used an old plastic placemat, cut down to a 290mm square – you will find the template for the crescent shape on our website. Glue the template to the mat with Spray Mount. Use a scalpel, and some kind of cutting board, to cut the two segments out of the plastic square as shown (fig.4).

Now turn to the next page to find out more...

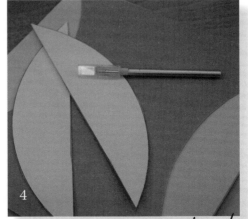

you can download this template from our website.

5

stencil the design
on in two sessions,
turning it ninety degrees
on the second run...

FAUX SPANISH TILES CONT'D...

It depends what surface you are tiling, but to fix the 'tiles' to the floor it would be best to, once again, line the floor with plywood sheeting. For maximum stability we would suggest using 18mm ply, but 12mm would probably be fine too. The varnish should dry to a wipeable and hard sealant, as with any painted floor. Maybe best not to combine it with stiletto heels, but normal usage should be perfectly fine...

Step 5.
Now you need to stencil your tiles — half of them in the lighter grey Zinc and half in the darker one, Fossil. Do the stencilling in two steps.

Step 6.
Place the stencil face down on the tile: it should be a little tacky from where you removed the template. Roll the paint over the gap, ensuring that you come off the stencil onto the board rather than paint towards it (that's how you prevent bleeding) (fig.5). Repeat with the other side and allow to dry (fig.6). Then repeat again to apply the design to the other two sides of the square. You should now have four crescents per tile. Do this for both colours.

Step 7.
Now varnish each square (top and sides) with an acrylic satin varnish, followed by a coat of Simply Varnish if you want a flatter appearance.

Step 8.
Glue the tiles in place onto the plywood floor with an instant grab adhesive like No More Nails. Use tile spacers or wooden tabs to create a uniform gap for the grout (fig.7).

Step 9.
Grout the tiles with a grey flexible tile grout which comes in powder form, mixed with water (fig.8), rather than use a ready-mixed variety.

Step 10.
Probably best to varnish the entire floor one more time, with either the satin or flat varnish.

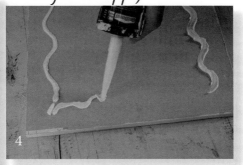

use a gun to apply the adhesive.

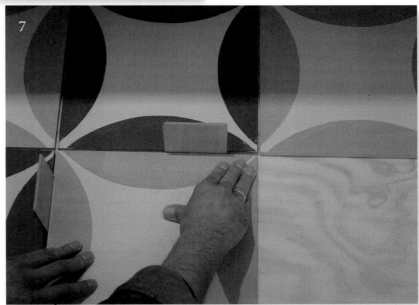

use tile spacers to lay the tiles neatly...

do not use ready mixed grout!

CLASSIC PAINTED CHECK FLOOR

Painted checked floors never seem tired or fall from fashion and they are relatively easy to achieve, providing your knees can take it! Also, you don't need to be a perfectionist to perform this task either – thankfully. As the floor is normally viewed from on high, the eye is very forgiving and absorbs the whole effect, rather than the details...

before you start, seal the original floor, with 2 coats of shellac to seal in any nasties...

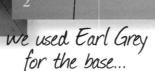

we used Earl Grey for the base...

we used Chape for the squares.

apply a wash of Sel de Mer to soften it down if needed, one part paint to two parts water.

Step 1.
After you have shellac'd the floor twice, paint two coats of your chosen base colour all over the floor, allowing each coat to dry before starting the next (fig.1).

Step 2.
Use a piece of card or an old box to make yourself a square template. Find a central line to work off and then draw the first square in pencil (fig 2). Using both the template and a long batten of wood, just keep extending the lines to make checks – using the template to keep it square. If you find you're going off centre, just re-draw the line and erase the first one. Draw a squiggle in pencil on all the squares you're going to paint in the darker colour.

Step 3.
Mask the outside of the squares to be painted (fig.3). Then with a mini roller and brush, carefully roll out the squares. Remember to always come off the tape onto the square, to avoid bleeding under the tape (fig.4).

Step 4.
Once dry, if the floor looks too sharp give the entire floor a quick wash with heavily diluted Sel de Mer paint to soften it down if needed (fig.5). Finally, apply at least one coat of acrylic satin varnish, plus a further coat of either satin or flat, depending on your choice (fig.6).

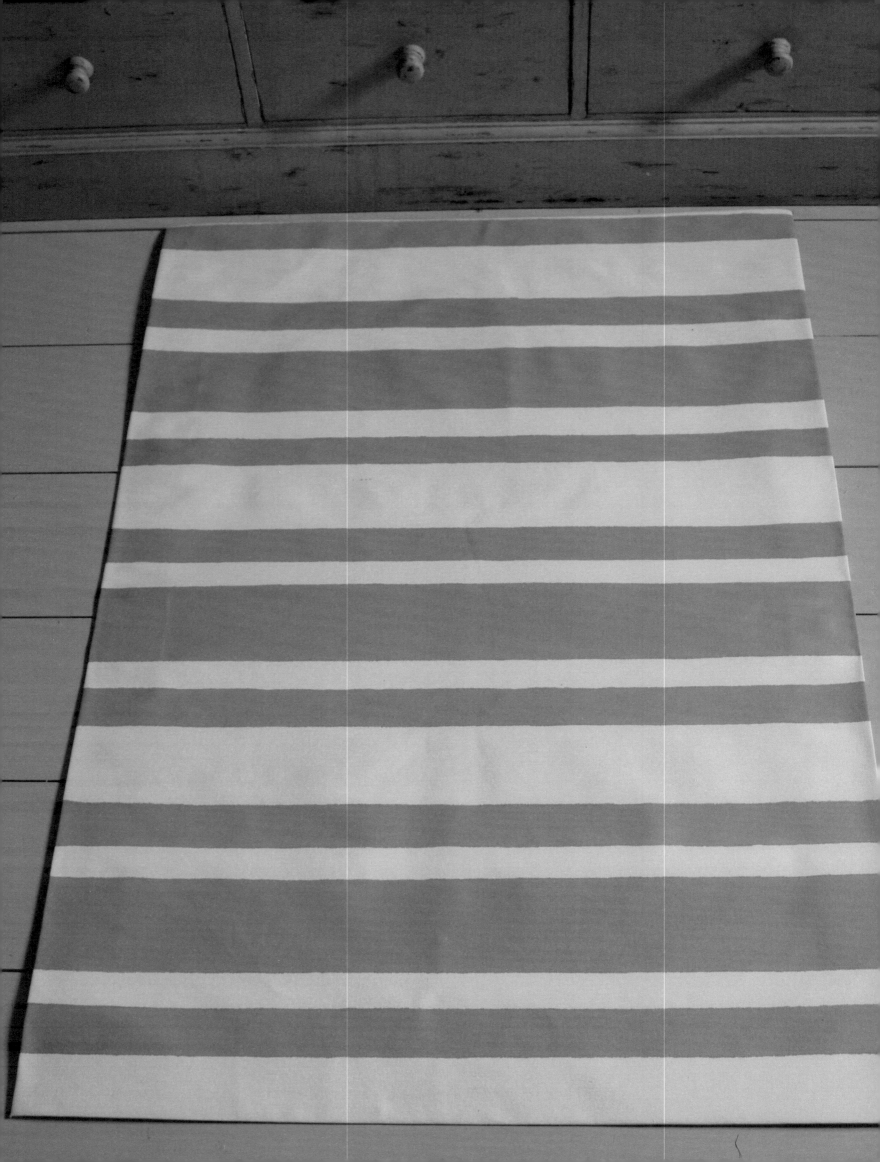

CANVAS FLOORCLOTH

Making your own floorcloth is a lot easier than you'd think.
Once again, as well as being a very inexpensive option, it
gives you the ability to create a bespoke piece
exactly to your own design and colour. Even better, it is
practical as well as good looking. The key ingredient is the
15oz cotton canvas, which we purchased from Whaleys
of Bradford – see page 168 for details.

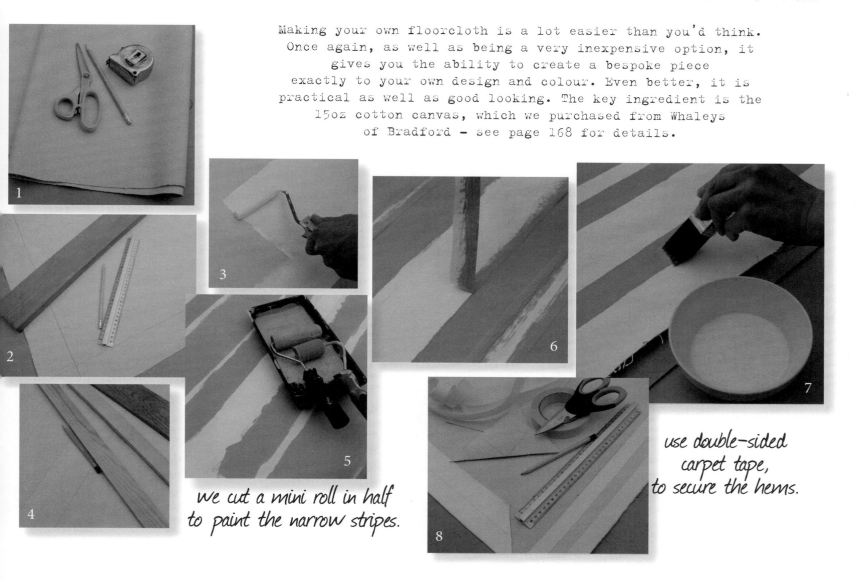

we cut a mini roll in half
to paint the narrow stripes.

use double-sided
carpet tape,
to secure the hems.

Step 1.
Cut your canvas to the required size, adding a 75mm hem all the way around (fig.1). Then draw
your hem in pencil all around the fabric (fig.2).

Step 2.
Now flip the fabric over and paint with two coats of an acrylic primer (fig.3). When dry use
three different sized planks to create stripes across the fabric. The gap between the large and
small stripes needs to be slightly smaller than the small stripe itself (fig.4).

Step 3.
Now mask the stripes with masking tape and then carefully roll the paint onto the masked
channels(fig.5). We used Hurricane for this project.

Step 4.
When completely dry, gently remove the masking tape. Small bleeds can be rectified by repairing
with more of the primer (fig.6). Then finish with two coats of our Simply Varnish (fig.7).

Step 5.
Flip the fabric over. Fold over the hem and crease. Cut the corners off and affix double-sided
carpet tape to the hem as shown – remove the protective paper and fold in place.

MOVING IMAGE

IMAGE TRANSFER

Of all the techniques we discovered whilst doing the research for this book, delving into the world of image transfer has been the most fascinating, and has enormous potential.

There are several ways to accomplish this technique yet they all seem to have drawbacks or, at the very least, unique characteristics that can restrict their usage or hamper their result. On balance, we think the version using an organic cleaning product from the USA, called Citra Solv, has the most universal appeal and works on wood, painted wood and, rather brilliantly, on fabric as well.

At the moment Citra Solv is not readily available in the UK but you can purchase it online. You need the concentrated cleaner and degreaser product, which has a pleasing Valencia Orange fragrance. It will seem expensive at first glance, but be assured that a little goes an awfully long way.

The next challenge is to find the right printer for the task. It has to be a laser printer as opposed to an inkjet one, and should be a toner-based system or copier – to be honest, the older the better. The kit used by swanky copy centres is likely to be too high spec for this, whereas an 'old faithful' down at the local store or library will probably be fine. We bought a Brother HL4150 from e-bay just for this task so try a little research online to source some more acceptable printers.

Once you've overcome these minor problems, the only limits will really be your imagination. Combined with some of the other skills we've imparted, you really can create all manner of beautiful *objets*.

We have to admit that it was some customers of ours who graciously shared their secrets to do with Image Transfer in the first place. They have asked to remain anonymous, but we've been hooked ever since, so we are eternally grateful for their kindness.

THE BASIC TECHNIQUE FOR WOOD...

First we'll start by showing you the basic technique for transferring onto wood. If using lettering, don't forget to reverse it first before you print it out. Most computer programmes will allow you to do this. If in doubt, ask your nearest teenager!

don't forget to reverse out the lettering before you start! we used a typeface called 'impact', another good one would be 'futura bold'.

Step 1.
Print out your reversed image and fix it securely in place, face down, with masking tape (fig.1). Position the tape so you can take a sneaky peek if needed.

Step 2.
Gently moisten a soft cloth in the Citra Solv, wiping off any excess, then dampen the lettering as shown (fig.2). Take care not to apply too much - the paper will turn transparent as you dampen.

Step 3.
Next, burnish the lettering carefully but quite firmly with the back of a spoon (fig.3) - you will need to apply a fair amount of pressure. Take a quick look without moving the paper too much. If all is fine, remove the paper, if not quite there, keep burnishing with the spoon. Et voila!

the most exciting moment - the reveal !

PROJECT: BREAD TRAY

THE BREAD TRAY
With your new skills, you can create all kinds of
stylish 'objets', from old signs to practical yet
good-looking containers and trays like this one.

we used our new colour Olive.

WHAT YOU'LL NEED...
1.8m piece of timber 65 x 14mm cut into
two pieces, each measuring 500mm long
and two approx. 400mm long.
7 pieces of batten 30 x 9 x 500mm.
Stain, shellac, paint and panel pins
Citra Solv for image transfer

you can download this lettering from our website.

we created a jig using some spare timber, to help with the assembly process.

Step 1.
Stain, shellac and one-colour age the four
side panels. Stain the thinner battens that
form the bottom of the tray (fig.1).

Step 2.
Image transfer the lettering onto the painted
panel following the previous instructions.
Apply one coat of varnish to seal (fig.2).

Step 3.
Loosely assemble the four side panels and
carefully nail the sides together using the
panel pins (fig.3).

Step 4.
Flip the frame over and nail in the bottom
slats, evenly spaced, starting at the ends
and working towards the centre (fig.4).

MY OLD DUTCH... CRATE.

Many years ago we used to drive to Holland regularly to buy our plants for the shops. On the way back, we used to visit an old friend who ran a truly inspiring brocante business in the countryside near Rotterdam. This project would make him smile...

image transfer as before...

does what it says on the bottle!

we used two pieces of 44 x 18 x 700mm and two 44 x 18 x 460mm for the side panels. Batten was made of fifteen pieces of 30 x 9 x 500mm.

Step 1.
Stain all the timber with our Simply Stain woodstain (fig.1). As you can see, it does what it says on the bottle!

Step 2.
Image transfer your lettering on the side panels as shown before (fig.2).

Step 3.
Assemble the side pieces and then carefully nail them together using some panel pins (fig.3).

Step 4.
Flip the frame over and make secure by nailing in the bottom battens, starting at the two edges and working inwards, leaving even spaces as you go (fig.4).

LUMIÈRES DE FÊTES

What could be more pleasing than these lovely
holiday lights glowing away on a summers evening.
Just use old wood and nails for candle-holders,
only of course, we've had to make the wood
look deliciously old first.

Step 1.
First either stain the wood with woodstain
or like these examples, age with vinegar.

Step 2.
Create your lettering and reverse out.When
the wood is ready, transfer your lettering
onto the panels as shown before (fig.2).

Step 3.
Mark where you want to fix the candles and
simply hammer in small nails from the
reverse (fig.3). We drilled pilot holes
but it is not essential. Add candles and
enjoy the ambience.

CRAQUELURE

Or should we say 'craqueleur', as the French would call it. This is an 'old favourite' technique in which the varnish cracks vaguely resembling an old master or genuine antique. Not to be confused with crackleglaze, where the paint itself cracks to reveal the colour below.

Craquelure has become even more appealing since we discovered the joys of image transfer. As you can clearly see, this old piece of scrap MDF has been transformed into something rather beautiful. The design possibilities are endless.

Thankfully, using the two-part system made for us by our friends at Polyvine, it is very easy to use and almost foolproof. The hardest bit is antiqueing up the cracks with the wax evenly, but even this is relatively straightforward. As you will see, all you do is paint on the base coat, allow to cure, then paint on the top coat. As it dries, completely random–sized tiny cracks appear all over the area you've painted. It's all so much easier than the methods we used years ago.

You can highlight the cracks using a combination of clear wax and brown wax. First apply the clear wax to allow you more time to work the brown wax when you apply it next, as these waxes dry very quickly. Removing the brown wax with a clean cloth and more of the clear wax, leaves behind a suitably impressive residue, suggesting an age gone by.

To our way of thinking, image transfer and craquelure were made for each other. Bravo!

IMAGE TRANSFER AND CRAQUELURE
WERE MADE FOR EACH OTHER...

CRAQUELURE

As we mentioned overleaf, Craquelure is where
the varnish cracks in tiny random pieces,
rather like the skin of a lizard. And although
it used to be tricky to use, this is no longer
the case. Now we use a two-part system, which
renders the process foolproof.
Just how we like it, eh?

*you can paint in random
directions but take care
not to overwork it...*

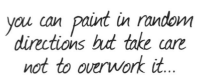

*you can see how the
varnish has cracked...*

you can always use raw umber as an alternative...

Step 1.
Firstly, transfer your image to the painted and distressed piece of MDF (fig.1) as shown before. NB: Do note that we heavily distressed the edges with a palm sander.

Step 2.
Paint on the base coat of the craquelure, it will be slightly luminous at first (fig.2). As it cures, it will become transparent. When completely clear and still a little tacky, you can apply the top coat. Random brush strokes are fine but don't overwork the piece. Allow to dry.

Step 3.
Now apply a coat of clear wax with a soft cloth (fig.3), swiftly followed by a second one, using the brown wax (fig.4).

Step 4.
Finally, clean off the brown wax with a fresh clean cloth and more of the clear wax (fig.5). The idea is to leave a residue of brown wax in the tiny cracks. Repeat as necessary and leave to dry overnight. Buff to a sheen with a clean cloth.

YOU CAN IMAGE TRANSFER ON FABRIC TOO...

TO TRANSFER ONTO FABRIC...

You do realise, of course, that if you master this technique, you have the ability you create your own fabric. Just how fabulous is that... And, even better, the finished designs are completely washable in a cool wash.

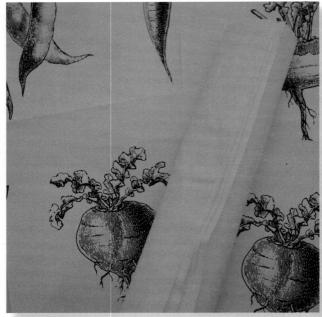

you can find plenty of copyright-free designs on the internet, or pay a small fee like we did...

we used very inexpensive white cotton from Whaleys of Bradford see back of book for details...

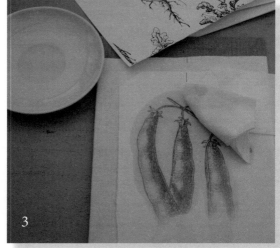

take care not to make the design too wet when using the Citra Solv.

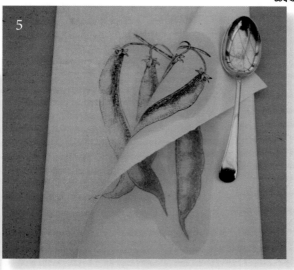

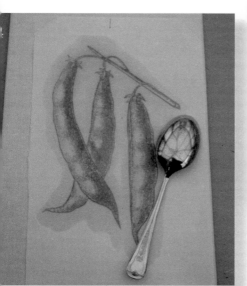

the world is now your proverbial oyster!

Step 1.
First of all, choose your design and print it out. Don't forget, if you're using text, to reverse it out (fig.1).

Step 2.
Firmly fix your fabric to a wooden board or similar with masking tape (fig.2). Place your design face down and tape in place. As before, try and to position it so you can take a quick look without moving the design.

Step 3.
Pour a small amount of Citra Solv in a saucer then, with a small piece of spare cotton, gently dampen the image as shown (fig.3). Do not over-wet the design. Once again, burnish it firmly with a spoon (fig.4). Check your image to see how you're doing (fig.5) and carry on burnishing if need be.

Step 4.
Remove the paper and discard. Allow to dry. Gently immerse in some cold water to clean off any excess Citra Solv. You should find that your design is completely colourfast. Allow to dry again, then iron with a spare piece of cotton on top of the fabric and then make into anything that takes your fancy.

SOME IDEAS FOR YOU...

As we said on the previous page, mastering this technique gives you unlimited possibilities. Here we show examples of cushions (fig.1), tea towel (fig.2), gorgeous elegant napkins (fig.3) and below, some coasters and tea napkins. Even more exciting is the fact that you can paint the designs a well, see the table mats o the right. Simply dilute th paint with a little water and off you go. The dilut- ed paint might bleed a lit tle, so put an absorbent pa of spare fabric underneath Then finally fix with a brief dip in cold water an wash in a cool wash.

1

2

3

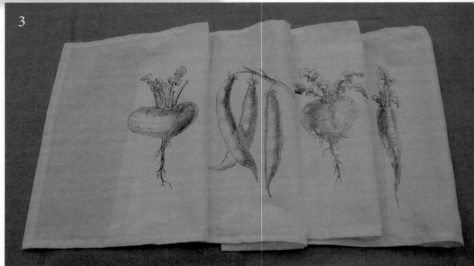

4

146

THE MOD PODGE METHOD...

Surely one of the strangest titles you're ever likely to see. Mod Podge is an American PVA glue with additives. This is another way to do Image Transfer and as it is very charming, we thought it deserved to be included. Once again, it will only work with toner-based laser printers or colour copiers.

you can find plenty of copyright-free designs on the internet.

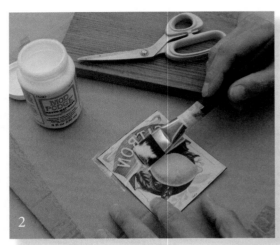

we aged the wood with vinegar beforehand.

Step 1.
Create your images as before, taking care to reverse out any text as shown (fig.1).

Step 2.
Paste the front of the image with a nice even coat of Mod Podge, don't be too sparing with the glue. Place on the wood and smooth out any bubbles with a dry cloth (fig.3).

Step 3.
Leave overnight to dry thoroughly. Use a damp sponge to moisten the image (fig.4) and then very gently rub with your finger to reveal the image (fig.5). Do this is in two or three stages, letting each one dry.

Step 4.
As you progress, the white residue (fig.6) will diminish. When enough of the image is revealed, apply one coat of Simply Varnish.

at each stage, the white residue will lessen.

GRAND ILLUSIONS
★

PAINT COURSES:
LEARN HOW TO GIVE YOUR FURNITURE, WALLS & FLOORS THAT CERTAIN 'JE NE SAIS QUOI..' ON OUR HIGHLY ACCLAIMED PAINT COURSES.

MOST OF OUR STOCKISTS RUN PAINT COURSES,
DO CHECK THE LIST ON PAGE 170 FOR YOUR NEAREST ONE...

GRAND ILLUSIONS
PAINT
VINTAGE plus+

GRAND ILLUSIONS

VINTAGE PAINT

PEINTUR

col.10 MOUSSE

col.11 MAROC

col.19 STOCKHOLM

col.20

AGE
NT
DE LAIT

AT. MATT PAINT
ORDIC-FRENCH
ND DESIGNED TO
TERMILK PAINTS
OTH CENT

contents

A range of 33 gorgeous colours inspired by a Nordic-French palette. These paints are available in 1-litre tins and 125ml pots for small projects, and are shown here one-colour aged and varnished with our new, improved Simply Varnish. Colours may be affected by the printing process. For best results, please refer to our hand-painted paint chart.

1.
SEL DE MER

2.
VANILLE

3.
LINEN

4.
CALICO

5.
EARL GREY

13.
PASTILLE

6.
SHUTTER

7.
ZINC

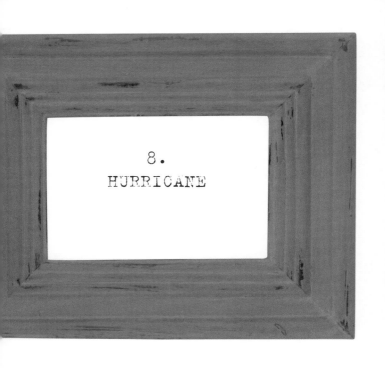

8.
HURRICANE

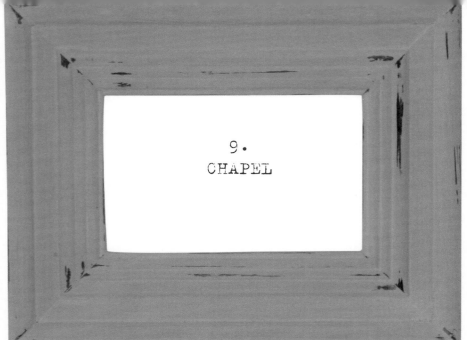

9.
CHAPEL

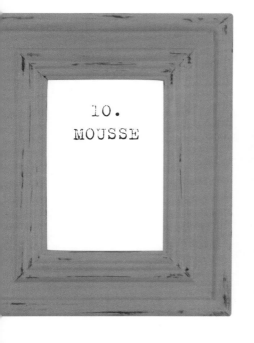

10.
MOUSSE

11.
MAROC

12.
DIJON

14.
FIGUE

16.
POWDER

15.
JUNIPER

17.
OPERA

18.
GULL'S EGG

19.
STOCKHOLM

20.
FJORD

21.
SUMMERHAUS

22.
GUSTAVIAN

23.
NORDIC BLUE

24.
VERDIGRIS

25.
CHARLESTON

26.
ARTICHAUT

27.
NOIR

29.
FOSSIL*

30.
GOTLAND*

28.
MENTHE*

33.
IONA*

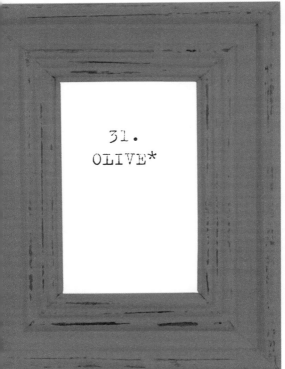

31.
OLIVE*

32.
VERDE*

* Limited Edition 2016

WATER BASED
WOODSTAIN

SHELLAC

ACRYLIC FLAT
VARNISH

CLEAR
WAX

BROWN
WAX

CRAQUELURE
SET

HAND PAINTED
PAINT CHART

PAINT BRUSHES
IN THREE SIZES

YOUR ONE-STOP SHOP!

MIXING COLOURS

Choosing chalk or milk paint colours can be quite difficult, especially when it comes to walls. It is the inherent soft matt texture of the paint which forms its beauty but which is also to some extent, its downfall. Due to their very flat matt finish, these paints absorb the light and, as such, can look completely different at various times of the day, or in different aspects of a room. This actually makes for a very satisfying effect, as the mood can change dramatically. The point is to be aware of this and really think about when you are planning to use the room, and to try a good sized sample and observe it throughout 24 hours at least, to be sure you are happy with the effect at all times of the day, including in bright sunlight. To be fair, this can probably be noticed with any flat paint, but see it as a positive rather than a negative, as it can make a room seem more alive.

In our case we deliberately chose to keep the range of colours quite small, for three very good reasons. Firstly, we do subscribe to the view that too much choice is not always a good thing, and certainly makes a decision even harder. Secondly, we want our stockists to carry sufficient stock so that they have the full range available at all times, which can be a large investment. We all know how irritating it is when having made the decision, your choice of colour is not there when you want it... And, finally, the third reason is because you can, of course, mix the paints which each other, to make a plethora of other colours. We have 33 colours in the collection at this time, yet armed with a can of Sel de Mer and Noir, you can make a further 99 glorious colours without needing to be a colour expert.

A small note of caution: it is only fair to say, that due to the anomalies of the photographic and then printing processes, the colours overleaf might not be quite as true as we would wish. They do give a good indication of course and you can clearly see the endless possibilities out there. One final point – if you are going to mix paint for a project, then do ensure you mix sufficient paint for the whole job before you start, and do record the recipe for future use. Also please note, our paints cannot be mixed with other types of paint.

Nbr. 1
Sel de Mer

10% Noir   20% Noir   30% Noir

Nbr. 2
Vanille

25% Sel de Mer   50% Sel de Mer   10% Noir

Nbr. 3
Linen

25% Sel de Mer   50% Sel de Mer   10% Noir

Nbr. 4
Calico

25% Sel de Mer   50% Sel de Mer   10% Noir

Nbr. 9
Chapel

25% Sel de Mer   50% Sel de Mer   10% Noir

THE NEUTRALS

Nbr. 5
Earl Grey

Nbr. 6
Shutter

Nbr. 7
Zinc

Nbr. 8
Hurricane

Nbr. 29
Fossil

25% Sel de Mer   25% Sel de Mer   25% Noir

25% Sel de Mer   50% Sel de Mer   50% Noir

25% Sel.de Mer   50% Sel de Mer   50% Noir

50% Sel de Mer   100% Sel de Mer   25% Noir

50% Sel de Mer   100% Sel de Mer   150% Sel de Mer

THE GREYS

Nbr. 18
Gulls Egg

25% Sel de Mer   50% Sel de Mer   10% Noir

Nbr. 19
Stockholm

25% Sel de Mer   50% Sel de Mer   10% Noir

Nbr. 20
Fjord

25% Sel de Mer   50% Sel de Mer   10% Noir

Nbr. 21
Summerhaus

25% Sel de Mer   50% Sel de Mer   10% Noir

THE BLUES

Nbr. 22
Gustavian

25% Sel de Mer *50% Sel de Mer* *75% Sel de Mer*

Nbr. 23
Nordic Blue

25% Sel de Mer *50% Sel de Mer* *75% Sel de Mer*

Nbr. 28
Menthe

25% Sel de Mer *50% Sel de Mer* *10% Noir*

Nbr. 33
Iona

25% Sel de Mer *50% Sel de Mer* *50% SdM 10% Noir*

MORE BLUES

Nbr. 13
Pastille

Nbr. 14
Figue

Nbr. 15
Juniper

Nbr. 16
Powder

Nbr. 17
Opera

25% Sel de Mer   50% Sel de Mer   10% Noir

THE MAUVY PINK RED SPECTRUM

Nbr. 10
Mousee

25% Sel de Mer *50% Sel de Mer* *25% Noir*

Nbr. 11
Maroc

25% Sel de Mer *50% Sel de Mer* *100% Sel de Mer*

Nbr. 12
Dijon

25% Sel de Mer *50% Sel de Mer* *15% Noir*

Nbr. 30
Gotland

25% Sel de Mer *50% Sel de Mer* *15% Noir*

EARTHY TONES

Nbr. 24
Verdigris

25% Sel de Mer   50% Sel de Mer   10% Noir

Nbr. 25
Charleston

25% Sel de Mer   50% Sel de Mer   10% Noir

Nbr. 26
Artichaut

25% Sel de Mer   50% Sel de Mer   10% Noir

Nbr. 31
Olive

25% Sel de Mer   50% Sel de Mer   10% Noir

Nbr. 32
Verde

25% Sel de Mer   50% Sel de Mer   10% Noir

THE SUBLIME GREENS

FREQUENTLY ASKED QUESTIONS....

SOMETIMES WHEN I VARNISH OR WAX MY PIECE SOME BROWN STAINING OCCURS, WHY IS THIS?
This is one of those random issues that happens every now and again - and it occurs with any brand of chalk or milk paint. As we mentioned earlier in the book, we prefer to teach prevention rather than cure. What happens is that when the varnish or wax is applied, in simple terms it passes through the paint to find the surface to adhere to. The paint is micro-porous as it is so soft and just occasionally this drags up a stain from beneath. That is why we recommend using shellac as a sealant at the start in some cases. Don't worry if it happens, you can cure this by applying two coats of shellac to the affected panel and then re-paint as before. For really stubborn staining (like oil for example) try using the acrylic primer Zinsser as this is shellac-based and the strongest we know. With upcycled items you never really know their history. The only other reason could possibly be that a) you didn't stir the varnish before use or b) you've left it out in the open and it is starting to cure. In the big scheme of things these issues are relatively rare.

CAN THE PAINT BE SPRAYED?
Yes, it can. You will need to dilute it a little with water to make it fluid enough to go through your spray gun.

CAN IT BE USED ON MELAMINE, MDF OR METAL?
Due to the fact Melamine has such a hard and slippery surface, we suggest you prime it first with an acrylic primer like Zinsser. MDF is perfectly fine and you should be able to paint straight from the can - no preparation required. Should also be fine on metal as it does possess good adhesion qualities but do be aware that this isn't its main purpose.

IS THE PAINT SUITABLE FOR FLOORS?
Yes, the paint is fine for floors but you need to treat the floor first with either two coats of shellac or the acrylic primer. Then apply at least two coats of the paint. When completely dry, apply one or two coats of acrylic satin varnish and then one or two of our new improved Simply Varnish to flatten it down if preferred.

HOW ABOUT USING THE PAINT OUTDOORS?
You can use the paint outdoors but you'll need to varnish it. It will then fade gracefully over time. For a longer lasting result, you'd need to find yourself an oil-based flat varnish.

WHAT ABOUT USING THE PAINT IN KITCHENS OR ON KITCHEN TABLES?
The number one enemy in kitchens is oily fingers. You might be wise to use a coat of acrylic satin varnish first, and then two coats of our Simply Varnish to flatten it down, although the latter is heat-resistant and water-resistant. We're just erring on the side of caution in case of heavy traffic, or if you have young children for example.

IS THE VARNISH HEAT-RESISTANT?
As discussed above, yes, in normal circumstances...

IS THE PAINT TESTED ON ANIMALS?
Absolutely not and it is also suitable for vegans too. Totally VOC free makes it a very eco-friendly paint indeed.

HOW LONG DOES THE PAINT TAKE TO DRY?
In normal climatic conditions the paint will dry very quickly - maybe 30 minutes to one hour. In the cold or damp a little longer.

CAN THE PAINTS BE MIXED?
Yes, they can be mixed with one another but not other brands or types of paint. Also, when using more than one can, always mix sufficient paint, for the whole task, in a larger container. Our paint is hand-made and made in batches - always check the batch number on the tin.

CAN YOU USE THE PAINT ON FABRIC?
As you will have seen in the book we have used the paint on fabric. As it is packed with natural pigments, it acts like a dye, but to avoid unwanted fabric stiffness, we diluted it in water a little. Once dry, after an initial rinse in cold water, it should be colourfast at a cool temperature. To be honest, while it would almost certainly work, we probably wouldn't suggest dyeing large pieces of fabric in the paint, for the simple reason that perfectly good fabric dyes are available, which would be a less expensive option.

IS THE PAINT AND VARNISH CHILD-SAFE?
As long as these are completely dry, then they are both child safe.

AND OTHER USEFUL INFORMATION.

FABRIC SUPPLIERS

The fabrics used in this book were purchased from:

WHALEYS (BRADFORD) LTD
HARRIS COURT
GREAT HORTON
BRADFORD
BD7 4EQ
www.whaleys.co.uk

We used:
Valencia Linen Natural
Matting Cotton White
Cotton Canvas 15oz

DOWNLOADABLE
COPYRIGHT FREE IMAGES

Try online with Google Images
and also go to:

www.thegraphicsfairy.com

This site has other useful information about
Image Transfer and the Copier/Printers usable.

TIMBER SUPPLIERS & CUTTING

During the process of creating this book we found that the best
DIY store was B&Q. They offer a wide range of timber but most
importantly, as we went to press, they offer free timber cutting.

www.diy.com

You may well find that your local timber yard
will be able to help too.

MOD PODGE

We obtained our Mod Podge from the following supplier:

YOUR DO IT YOURSELF CENTRE LTD
33 ST JOHNS WAY
CORRINGHAM
ESSEX
SS17 7NA
www.yourdiycentre.co.uk

Other stockists are available online.

---

www.grandillusions.co.uk

For more information about our products, the
paint and the sundry items, please go to our
website. Here, you will be able to download
any templates used in the book and at some
point in the future, find information and
links to short videos online, demonstrating
some of the techniques used here.

GRAND ILLUSIONS
BLYNFIELD STOUR ROW SHAFTESBURY SP7 0QW ENGLAND
Tel: +44 (0) 1747 858300
E: sales@grandillusions.co.uk

PAINT STOCKISTS

BEDFORDSHIRE
Room no 9
5A High Street
Leighton Buzzard
LU7 1DN
T: 01528 852741

Soper & Co
8 High Street
Toddington
LU5 6BY
T: 01525 877164

BERKSHIRE
Antique Rose
3 Bush Walk
Wokingham
RG40 1AT
T: 01189 798414

Huttons
77 Peascod Street
Windsor
SL4 1DH
T: 0208 876 2761

BUCKINGHAMSHIRE
Moss
9 Cornwall Place
High Street
Buckingham
MK18 1SB
T: 01280 821314

CAMBRIDGESHIRE
Beautiful Swagger
56b High Street
St Neots
PE19 1JG
T: 0845 5196216

Hazelmere Home & Garden
2 Great Whyte
Ramsey
PE26 1HA
T: 01487 711432

CAMBRIDGESHIRE cont'd...
Providence
Burwash Manor
New Road
Barton
CB23 7EY
T: 01223 264666

CARDIFF
Annie & Co
11 High Street
Cardiff
CF10 1AW
T: 07760 994929

Bodlon
12 Park Road
Whitchurch
CF14 7BQ
T: 02920 650564

CARMARTHENSHIRE
Leekes Dept Store
Business Park
Cross Hands
SA14 6RB
T: 0333 222 4120

Ruby's Yard
Sycamore Street
Newcastle Emlyn
SA38 9AJ
T: 0749 8856285

CHESHIRE
Nichols & Co (Chester) Ltd
5 Bridge Street Row East
Chester
CH1 1NW
T: 01244 322812

Okells Garden Centre Ltd
Duddon Heath
Nr Tarpoley
CW6 0EP
T: 01829 741512

Strippadoor
Unit 8 , Victoria Dye Works
Hempshaw Lane
Stockport
SK1 4LG
T:01614 778980

CHESHIRE cont'd...
The Lavender Tree
103–105 Brook Lane
Alderley Edge
SK9 7RU
T: 01625 599532

Vintage Angel Design
Unit 5 Stamford House
Moss Lane
Altrincham
WA14 2PU
T: 01619 290446

CORNWALL
Blue Buoy Trading
The Bay Box
5 Brentwartha
Polperro
PL13 2RL
T: 01503 272085

Camellia Interiors
3E Treloggan Industrial Estate
Newquay
TR7 2SX
T: 01637 854304

Just Delights Cornwall Ltd
Commercial Road
Penryn
TR10 8AQ
T: 01326 379075

Uneeka Home ltd
Princess Chula House
City Road
Truro
TR1 2JL
T: 01872 888538

CUMBRIA
Armstrong Ward
8 Wainwrights Yard
Kendal
LA9 4DP
T: 01539 720400

Parma Violet
45 Main Street
Kirkby Lonsdale
LA6 2AH
T: 01524 212585

CUMBRIA
Squirrel
43 Market Street
Ulverston
LA12 7LS
T: 01229 588028

DERBYSHIRE
Bottle Kiln Retail Ltd
The Bottle Kiln
High Lane
West Hallam
DE7 6HP
T: 0115 932 9442

Dallies Chic Interiors
78 King Street
Alfreton
DE55 7DD
Derbyshire
T: 01773 836020

Fairways Garden Centre
Clifton Ashbourne
DE6 2GN
Derbyshire
T: 01335 347900

Heritage Paint Centre
Bath Street
Bakewell
DE45 1BX
Derbyshire
T: 01629 812223

Quintessentially Vintage
2 Coldwell Street
Wirksworth
DE4 4FB
T: 01629 820191

DEVON
Beaux Cadeaux Ltd
33 The Broadway
Plymstock
Plymouth
PL9 7AF
T: 01752 961600

Brocante 66
The Narrows
66 High Street
Totnes
TQ9 8SQ
T: 01803 840010

DEVON cont'd...
Coastline Gifts and Interiors
3 Rolle Street
Exmouth
EX8 1HL
Devon
T: 01395 227 40

az Interiors
16 Fore Street
vybridge
PL21 9AB
T: 01752 894012

Scuffle and Jones
03 High Street
Crediton
EX17 3LF
T: 0772 0659687

Strummer Pink
57 High Street
Honiton
EX14 1LJ
T: 01414 758030

DORSET
Antelope Gallery
Antelope Walk
Dorchester
DT1 1BE
T: 01305 260437

Gray's
High Street
Stalbridge
DT10 2LJ
Dorset
T: 01963 365800

The Shabby Chic Shack
27 Belle Vue Road
Southbourne
BH6 3DJ
T: 01202 430801

DUMFRIES & GALLOWAY
Rhubarb
5 St Mary Street
Kirkudbright
DG6 4AA
T: 01557 339286

DYFED
Seld Interiors
4 Bridge Street
Aberaeron
SA46 0AR
T: 01654 767475

EAST MIDLANDS
Rutland Interiors & Upholstery
The Conservatories
Rutland Village
Ashwell Road
Oakham
Rutland
LE15 7QN
T: 01572 756660

EAST SUSSEX
Banana Tree
2 Grove Road
Eastbourne
BN21 4TJ
T: 01323 647713

Shop
32-34 Norman Road
St Leonards on Sea
TN38 0EJ
T: 01424 713868

ESSEX
Chloe Elizabeth
59 Broadway West
Leigh on Sea
SS9 2BX
T: 01702 470331

Potty Moo's
Ford Farm
Braintree Road
Dunmow
CM6 1HU
T: 01371 876 385

Potty Moo's
20 High Street
Saffron Walden
CB10 1AX
T: 01799 513682

Your Do It Yourself Centre Ltd
33 St John's Way
Corringham
SS17 7NA
T: 01375 673014

FLINTSHIRE
Abakhan Fabrics
Coast Road
Llanerch-y-Mor
Mostyn
CH8 9DX
T: 01745 562100

GLOUCESTERSHIRE
Cornflower and Calico
Unit 2 , 50 High Street
Stroud
GL5 1AN
T: 01453 757336

Les Roses
2 Cheltenham Road
Stratton
Cirencester
GL7 2HX
T: 01285 650691

Pink Vintage
10 Rotunda Terrace
Montpellier St
Cheltenham
GL50 1SW
T: 01242 463008

Vintage-en-vogue
The Shed Antique Centre
Stratford Road
Mickleton
GL56 6SR
T: 07717 615298

GREATER MANCHESTER
The Restoration House
62 Market Street
Tottington
Bury
BL8 3LJ
T: 01204 8800889

HAMPSHIRE
Distinctive Design Ltd
4 Warwick Lane
3-4 The Square
Wickham
PO17 5JN
T: 01329 833864

HAMPSHIRE cont'd...
One of a Kind
Royal Clarence Marina
Unit 7 Weevil Lane
North Meadow
Gosport
PO12 1BP
Hampshire
T: 02392 177172

Overton Gallery
20 High Street
Overton
RG25 3HA
Hampshire
T: 01256 773143

Shave Green Interiors
70 High Street
Lyndhurst
SO43 7BJ
Hampshire
T: 02380 283915

HEREFORDSHIRE
No 28 Fabrics and Interiors
28 Church Street
Hereford
HR1 2LR
T: 01432 272898

Shed
Holling Grange
Abbey Dore
Hereford
HR2 0JJ
T: 01981 241531

HERTFORSHIRE
Chalk and Stone at Room 89,
10 Union Street
Barnet
EN5 4HZ
T: 07739 186916

H@me & Eat
Unit 3 Birchanger Ind Estate
Bishops Stortford
CM23 2TH
T: 01279 814644

ISLE OF WIGHT
Staples & Green
13A Shooters Hill
Cowes
PO31 7BG
Isle of Wight
T: 01983 294958

PAINT STOCKISTS

JERSEY
Mark Howe Flowers Ltd
4 West Street
St Helier
JE2 4ST
Jersey
T: 01534 618920

KENT
Artisan for Unusual Things
80 London Road
Teynham
ME9 9QH
T: 01795 522121

Avery Interiors
54-56 High Street
West Wickham
BR4 0NH
T: 0208 777 7360

French.. Inspired Interiors
67 Oxford Street
Whitstable
CT5 1DA
Kent
T: 01227 634138

Paramor Boorman Home
16 Westcliff Road
Ramsgate
CT11 0JD
T: 01843 597571

Queen Bee Home
12 Mercery Lane
Canterbury
CT1 2JJ
T: 01227 471025

LANCASHIRE
Maison Interiors
1-6 York Street
Clitheroe
BB7 2DL
Lancashire
T: 01200 427007

LEICESTERSHIRE
All Things Bright & Beautiful
33 High Street
Waltham on the Wold
Melton Mowbray
LE14 4AH
Leicestershire
T: 07510 915 844

Browse Interiors
35 Station Road
Lutterworth
LE17 4AP
T: 01455 559 639

Gallery 18
18A Churchgate
Loughborough
LE11 1UD
T: 01509 232347

Gloss Interiors
6 Bath Street Corner
Ashby de la Zouch
LE65 2FH
T: 01530 588594

Lavender Blue
15 Church Street
Market Harborough
LE16 7AA
T: 01858 419090

Michaelmas House
4 Main Street
Market Bosworth
Nr Nuneaton
CV13 0JW
T: 01455 291303

Outerspace Home & Garden Ltd
rear of 43-45 Francis Street
Stoneygate
Leicester
LE2 2BE
T: 01162 745502

Outerspace Home & Garden Ltd
Wistow Rural Centre
Kibworth Road
Wistow
Leicester
LE8 8QF
T: 0116 259 2467

LINCOLNSHIRE
Flowers 'n' Things
3 Red Lion Street
Spalding
Lincs
PE11 1SX
T: 01775 769306

Ruddocks
287 High Street
Lincoln
LN2 1AW
Lincolnshire
T: 01522 528285

LONDON
Les Sardines
42 Queenstown Road
Battersea
SW8 3RY
T: 0207 738 8499

Luma
98 Church Road
Barnes
SW13 0DQ
T: 0208 748 2264

Penny 2 Feathers
120 Columbia Road
E2 7RG
T: 0207 739 7103

Room Remedies
12 Lambton Road
Raynes Park
SW20 0LR
T: 0208 946 6894

Three Four Five
345 Portobello Road
W10 5SA
T: 0208 960 3051

MERSEYSIDE
Angels of Churchtown
50 Botanic Road
Churchtown
Southport
PR9 7NE
T: 01704 509811

MIDDLESEX
Attic
34-36 High Street
Hampton Hill
TW12 1PD
T: 0208 943 9626

NORFOLK
Alfie's Emporium
The Phoenix Studio
The Turning Point
Beeston Regis
Sherringham
NR26 8TS
T: 01263 515595

Country Modern
Nowhere Lane
Great Witchingham
NR9 5PD
T: 01603 554224

Grubby Green
The Vintage Market
2A Queens Road
Norwich
NR1 3PR
T: 01603 623111

Home by Annie Lambert
The Courtyard
Creake Abbey
North Creake
Fakenham
NR21 9LF
Norfolk
T: 07796 656 384

Wiggle Room Stuff
Bulldog Barns,
14 Thetfold Road
Northwold
Thetford
IP26 5LS
T: 07904 508444

NORTH LINCOLNSHIRE

The Gallery
Something Old, Something New
15 George Street
Barton upon Humber
North Lincs
DN18 5ES
T: 01652 408060

NORTH YORKSHIRE

Greyhound Antiques
58 Market Place
Malton
YO17 7LW
T: 07957 232 973

Signz Interiors
8/9 Holmbeck Road
Skelton in Cleveland
Cleveland
TS12 2AL
T: 01287 654700

NORTHAMPTONSHIRE

Genevieve
5 The Jamb
Corby Old Village
Corby
NN17 1AY
T: 01536 443744

Inside Out (Towcester)
9 White Horse Yard
Towcester
NN12 6BU
T: 01327 359577

Romejos
14 Market Place
Oundle
PE8 4BQ
T: 01832 272165

Vintage French Lifestyle
114A Kingsley Park Terrace
Northampton
NN2 7HU
T: 01604 713227

NOTTINGHAMSHIRE

Glorious Homes
50 Station Road
Sandiacre
Nottingham
NG10 5AS
T: 0115 939 4081

NOTTINGHAMSHIRE

Henry Brewer Gallery
3 Tudor Square
West Bridgeford
NG2 6BT
T: 0115 981 1623

Uplifting Gifts
47 Main Street
Burton Joyce
Nottingham
NG14 5DR
T: 01159 262303

ORKNEY

The Quernstone
38 Victoria Street
Stromness
KW16 3AA
Orkney
T: 01856 852 900

OXFORDSHIRE

Heart and Soul
Unit 1A Manor Farm
Northampton Road
Weston on the Green
Bicester
OX25 3QL
T: 07749 298141

Lily's Attic
51 B Market Square
Witney
OX28 6AG
T: 01993 771273

PEMBROKESHIRE

The Golden Sheaf Gallery
25 High Street
Narbeth
SA67 7AR
T: 01834 860407

POWYS

Kitty Keane Vintage
North House
St Mary's Street
Brecon
LD3 7AA
T: 01874 623849

Nicholls Crickhowell
19 High Street
Crickhowell
NP8 1BD
T: 01873 811605

POWYS cont'd...

The Deco Shop
35-37 Heol Maengwyn
Machynllth
SY20 8EB
T: 01654 700001

Workhouse Gallery
Industrial Estate
Presteigne
LD8 2UF
T: 01544 267864

RHONDDA CYON TAFF

Leekes Llantrisant Dept Store
Cowbridge Road
Pontyclun
Llantrisant
CF72 8XU
T: 0333 222 4120

SOMERSET

Bare and Willow
c/o Nickys Flower Studio
Riverside Place
Taunton
TA1 1JJ
T: 01823 288289

Home Front
10 Margaret's Building
Brock Street
Bath
BA1 2LP
T: 01225 571711

Sharpham Park Retail
The Great House
Kilver Court
Shepton Mallet
T: 01749 340417

The Home Specialist
Farleigh Road Farm Shop
Norton St Philip
Bath
BA2 7NG
T: 012225 723242

SOUTH YORKSHIRE

French Affair
The Chapel
99 Broadfield Road
Sheffield
S8 0XH
T: 0114 2588288

STAFFORDSHIRE

Sweet Little Ltd
56&58 Main Street
Barton under Needwood
DE13 8AA
T: 01283 712799

STIRLING

Green Pea Studio
Blaircessnock
Port of Menteith FK8 3JZ
Stirling
T: 0774 9198 521

SUFFOLK

A G Lifestyle
36-38 Station Road
Sudbury
CO10 2SS
T: 01787 312126

Panache Home and Accessories
Unit rear of Chestnut House
Wilby Road
Stradbridge
IP21 5JP
T: 01379 388735

Snape Maltings Retailing
Snape Bridge
Snape
IP17 1SR
T: 01728 688303

The Leaping Hare Country Store
Wyken Vineyards
Stanton
Bury St Edmunds
IP33 2DW
T: 01359 250262

Vintage Treasures
12 Bury Street
Stowmarket
IP14 1HA
T: 07517 373518

PAINT STOCKISTS

SURREY
Hatton Hill
41 High Street
Bagshot
GU19 5AF
T: 01276 476794

One Forty
140 High Street
Cranleigh
GU6 8RF
T: 01483 272627

Shabby Chic Country Living
62A West Street
Dorking
RH4 1BS
T: 01306 880626

The Packhouse Ltd
Hewetts Kiln
Tongham Road
Farnham
GU10 1PJ
T: 01252 781010

SWANSEA
Oyster Gallery Ltd
70-72 Newton Road
Mumbles
SA3 4BE
T: 01792 366988

TYNE & WEAR
Cleadon Antiques and Gifts
39 Front Street
Cleadon
Sunderland
SR6 7PG
T: 0191 5194444

VALE OF GLAMORGAN
Miss Holmes
11 High Street
Barry
CF62 7DZ
T: 01446 732456

Number 39
39 High Street
Cowbridge
CF71 7AE
Vale of Glamorgan
T: 01446 677380

WEST MIDLANDS
Archies Attic
Garden Village
Bridgenorth Road
Wolverhampton
West Midlands
WV6 7EZ
T: 07896 303163

Oopsy Daisies
Unit 61A
Merry Hill Shopping Centre
Brierley Hill
DY5 1QX
T: 01384 936310

Heritage Rooms
Mitchells
Unit 1 Weeford Road
Sutton Coldfield
B75 6NA
T: 0121 308 1679

La Boutique Bo-M
58 Melrose Ave
Stourbridge
DY8 2LE
T: 07921 555879

Leekes Coventry Dept Store
Silverstone Drive
junction 3 of the M6
Coventry
CV6 6PA
T: 0333 222 4120

Leekes Bilston Dept Store
Great Bridge Road
Bilston
Wolverhampton
WV14 8LB
T: 0333 222 4120

WEST SUSSEX
Arundel Interiors
67-69 Tarrant Street
Arundel
BN18 9DN
T: 01903 368 284

WEST SUSSEX cont'd...
Home to Roost
The Old Wagon Shed
Sandhills Farm
Sandhills Lane
Washington
RH20 4TD
West Sussex
T: 01903 893685

Oakapple Trading Company
Golden Square
Petworth
GU28 0AP
West Sussex
T: 01798 342576

Rocking Horse Antiques &
Home
15-17 Martlets Shopping Centre
Burgess Hill
RH15 9NN
T: 01444 244507

Tufnells Interiors Ltd
59 High Street
Lindfield
RH16 2HN
T: 01444 483483

WEST YORKSHIRE
Daisy Days
56 Main Street
Haworth
BD22 8DP
West Yorkshire
T: 01535 644653

Kooky Blue
42 Station Road
Ossett
WF5 8AY
West Yorkshire
T: 01924 265604

Snug
77 Lidget Street
Lindley
Huddersfield
HD3 3JP
T: 01484 644411

WILTSHIRE
First-View Gallery
Spread Eagle Courtyard
NT Stourhead
BA12 6QE
T: 01747 840747

Leekes Dept Store
Beanacre Road
Melksham
Wiltshire
SN12 8AG
T: 0333 222 4120

WORCESTERSHIRE
St Richard's Hospice
Lowesmoor Homestore
39/41 Lowesmoor
Worcester
WR1 2RS
T: 01905 763963

**DO CHECK THE WEBSITE FOR THE
LATEST LIST OF STOCKISTS.**

merci

First of all, we'd like to thank Gin, Geoff and Sam Hayward for believing in us and investing significantly in the brand. The company has grown enormously in the past four years, including the relaunch of our wonderful paint. None of this would have been possible without your support, so thank you.

To the incredible editors Jo and Meryl, fountains of knowledge as ever and graciously sharing their talents with us. Debs and Alistair of Attic, without whose generosity chapter two would have been very different indeed. And of course dear Emily, who wrote such a lovely foreword for us.Very special thanks to Chris, Rachel, Jill and Tony for reasons we cannot say, but you know why... Dan, Gavin, Chris and Ellie for invaluable help in the photographic department. Ali and Justin for the website.

Again, more special thanks to the GI teams over the years, in London and Dorset, who keep us going each and every day — right now this means, Debbie, Dottie, Zoe, Becci, Tracy x 2, Sarah, Lynn, Jordan, Glenn, Iain, Terry, Jean, the show production team and of course dear Suzanne, who not only has to put up with our nonsense daily, she also did the sewing!

Family and friends, not least but including Susan, Robert, Jonathan, Rowena, Linda & Johnny.

And finally, most important of all, to you our customers past and present, especially the ever-growing band of paint stockists — none of this would be possible without your support, so thank you!

If we have forgotten anyone, please forgive us...
To be launching this book on the eve of the 30th anniversary of the founding of Grand Illusions is incredibly fitting.

Nick & David x